PLANT SPIRIT
JOURNEY

About the Author

Laura Silvana is a truly remarkable visionary and mystic. She has explored the spiritual realms through profound mystical experiences and communications with souls beyond the veil. She is best known for her work as a spiritual intuitive, a healing medium, and a counselor of the soul. Her mediumship presented itself early in childhood, passed on to her through her family lineage. Her written works include *The Light of God* (published under Laura Aversano), a book that explores the nature of God and the soul in alignment with mystical Christianity, and *The Divine Nature of Plants* (out of print), a book that also explores the subject of plant spirit healing and medicine.

Laura's education includes both personalized training with psychic and spiritual healers and formal studies in energy medicine. Her trainings include applied kinesthesiology, polarity energy medicine, shamanism, and cranial sacral work, along with extensive training in spiritual counseling and development. She utilizes her gift of communicating with the other side, combined with her education, to help people of all walks of life and spirit. Her clients come from across the United States and all over the world, and there are many testimonials to her work.

You can visit Laura on her website, www.LauraSilvanaAversano.com or www.LauraAversano.com.

～ *Laura Silvana*

PLANT SPIRIT
JOURNEY

DISCOVER THE HEALING ENERGIES
OF THE NATURAL WORLD

Llewellyn Publications
Woodbury, Minnesota

First Edition
First Printing, 2009

Book design by Steffani Sawyer
Cover art ©2004 Visual Language®
Cover design by Ellen Dahl

Llewellyn is a registered trademark of Llewellyn Worldwide, Ltd.

Library of Congress Cataloging-in-Publication Data
Aversano, Laura, 1970–
   Plant spirit journey : discover the healing energies of the natural
world / Laura Silvana Aversano.—1st ed.
      p. cm.
   ISBN 978-0-7387-1863-7
   1. Spiritual healing. 2. Medicinal plants. 3. Nature, Healing power of.
4. Shamanism. I. Title.
   BF1045.M44A94 2009
   133'.258—dc22
                              2009025461

Llewellyn Worldwide does not participate in, endorse, or have any authority or responsibility concerning private business transactions between our authors and the public.

All mail addressed to the author is forwarded but the publisher cannot, unless specifically instructed by the author, give out an address or phone number.

Any Internet references contained in this work are current at publication time, but the publisher cannot guarantee that a specific location will continue to be maintained. Please refer to the publisher's website for links to authors' websites and other sources.

Note: The author and publisher of this book are not responsible in any manner whatsoever for any injury that may occur through following the instructions contained herein. The recipes and remedies in this book are not meant to diagnose, treat, prescribe, or substitute for consultation with a licensed health-care professional. They are not for commercial use or profit. New herbal remedies should always be taken in small amounts to allow the body to adjust and to test for possible allergic reactions.

Llewellyn Publications
A Division of Llewellyn Worldwide, Ltd.
2143 Wooddale Drive, Dept. 978-07387-1863-7
Woodbury, Minnesota 55125-2989, U.S.A.
www.llewellyn.com

Printed in the United States of America

Acknowledgments

I will keep this simple. My gratitude to my family, and to the lessons we have had to learn in order to grow, heal, and love one another. May those lessons continue throughout time. To my mentors, John B. and Father Joe. My heartfelt appreciation for your continued faith in me and my work; your love and support have kept me going. I thank God often for bringing both of you into my life. And to the dear friends who have held me when I needed it; you know who you are. Thank you for being there.

My appreciation to those at Llewellyn who made this book possible, especially Cat and Sandy. Thank you for your direction, support, and guidance. It has been a pleasure working with you.

To My Animal Companions:

Alexis, you sweet and gentle soul. You visit from heaven often. I can see you beyond the veil, still resting your head against the pillow you called your own. You walk through our home, your petite body free of pain now, still playing with the spirits who love you so. You were very much a part of the writing of this book. I am grateful to all the souls and elementals who helped you transition.

Ceara, my little healer, my twin soul. You had enormous strength and courage while you were here on earth. You proved to be a miracle to modern veterinary medicine, surviving acute cancer seven years ago. You are indeed a testament to the workings of plant spirit medicine, prayer, healing, and the benevolence of the spirit world. You crossed over just after the writing of this book, continuing to do the work that you were meant for. I see you often, as I do Alexis, your body also free from suffering and existing as pure love.

Both of your courageous spirits will endure forever.

CONTENTS

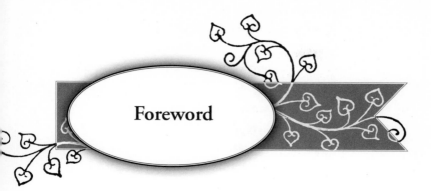

Foreword

It is said that the Buddha once gave a sermon without saying a word; he merely held up a flower to his listeners. I am sure Ms. Silvana was in the audience and listening to every word of the Buddha's flower. *Plant Spirit Journey* is about the art of listening to the spirit essence of each plant. The alchemists called this type of intuitive listening the "law of signatures," and shamans from all indigenous cultures have learned the art of plant knowledge directly from the plants.

When I read Ms. Silvana's writing, I am reminded of William Blake's poem:

> *To see a world in a grain of sand*
> *and heaven in a wildflower,*
> *hold infinity in the palm of your hand*
> *and eternity in an hour.*

And like William Blake's words, her plant spirit prayers rise to the intensity of poetry to communicate the highest essence of each plant.

In the spirit of Dr. Edward Bach and his discovery of the Bach flower remedies, Ms. Silvana honors each aspect of every plant. She listens on many levels and integrates, with ease, her vast intuitive abilities with her knowledge of energy medicine and shamanism. She allows the message of the whole plant to come forward for body, mind, and spirit.

Plant Spirit Journey is a remarkable work of intuitive listening. Ms. Silvana artfully draws us into a world where plants are animated and intelligent beings. Her words are like conduits for the energy of the plants to come to the reader. Something awakens inside of us, and reading and plant healing become one.

—Dr. John Beaulieu, ND, PhD, Author of *Music and Sound in the Healing Arts, The Polarity Therapy Workbook,* and *The Seven Levels of a Still Point*

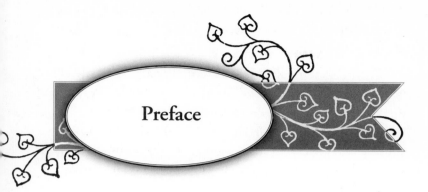

Preface

My communication with souls on the other side, and our united desire to share this marvelous, wisdom-embracing plant spirit medicine with others, is what led me to write this book. In it you will find the story of my journey, as well as intimate details involving my friends and teachers in the spirit world. You'll read about how I learned to work with plant spirit medicine, and how its magic helped both myself and others through difficult times. Following that is a special guide to some of the plants I have worked with over the years to nurture myself, my friends, my family, and my clients. The healing therein will open your heart and mind to a new way of respecting the healing that the natural world has waiting for you.

Because of my energetic sensitivities and high frequencies, my physical body has been plagued by various ailments since I was a child. Traditional medicine only helped in part. As my relationship with the spirit world grew, so did my understanding of healing and the natural remedies that were imparted to me. I discovered that my life was not my own, in a way, since every experience was leading me closer to my destiny. I eventually came to recognize and align myself with the truth: that I was here to serve, to learn how to heal myself and be of assistance to others.

There is a special moment when you realize that there is a distinction between the heavenly world and its spirits, who roam freely, and the earth plane that we physically inhabit. That moment came for me as a child. Intrigued by spirits, I befriended many at a very impressionable age; some of those spirits later became my allies as I was groomed for what has turned out to be an unimaginable life...a life filled with magic and healing, sorrow and strife, blessing and grace. A life that has embraced many spiritual and physical initiations, starting at the beginning many times over, and on many different levels.

My Journey

The Beginning...

When I was a little girl, I would play in the alcove atop my bedroom closet. I often used to think that I was dreaming while awake, since I would see and speak with people that no one else in the house seemed even to notice. I remember telling my mom about my special friends, especially the Native American ones, who would visit and play with me.

By the time I was six or seven, I had developed a keen interest in the afterlife and in souls who could speak and connect with us from beyond the veil. I remembered lives I'd lived before, and told my mom how I'd died in some of them. My curiosity about psychic phenomena was beginning to develop, and I am grateful to have had a mother who was gifted as well.

I was plagued with a number of ailments as a child, one of which almost took my life at the age of eight. I had pneumonia and a collapsed lung, and was hospitalized for a number of weeks while antibiotics failed to alleviate any of the symptoms that presented themselves. That illness set a precedent for what would be a number of challenging physical conditions throughout my life, conditions that were initiated by the spirit world.

In energy medicine, a "miasm" is an imbalance in the energy field. It can interrupt or corrupt any variable that leads to healing. Miasms can travel with us through various incarnations, and some are passed down in the ancestral DNA of a person's spiritual, emotional, and physical energetic matrix. It is my belief, from years of working with spirits and with clients in my healing practice, that imbalances in the energy field can come from various dimensions and understandings in the spirit world. At the appropriate time and place in a person's life, they will be reconciled.

My miasm was already firmly established by the time I was rushed to the hospital one cold evening in New York City. My heart rate was slow, and I was barely breathing due to the fluid that filled my lungs. I remember being disoriented as nurses and doctors pulled me from the arms of my mother's friend, who was carrying me. Limp and feeling forlorn, I held on to my mother's hand as I drifted into the ethers. I remember the doctors working to find a vein to draw some blood for testing.

I knew that besides my parents, there were other souls around me, ones that no one else could see. And somehow, in the midst of all that chaos, I knew that I would be all right. I had to be. My mother and her father, my grandfather, both had had a spiritual sickness that manifested itself when they were young. As was the case with me, the traditional route to healing was of little avail for them.

As my mother remembers the story from her native Sicily, my grandfather fell ill at a very young age. His symptoms mimicked a coma in today's pathology, but back then all the local doctor knew was that there was a young boy who would not wake up. After every method of waking my grandfather failed, a decision was made to call the witch doctor who lived on that part of the island. After many prayers, and with my grandfather still in a coma, the witch doctor summoned my grandfather to get up and get one of the family's chickens, cut off its head, and then to come back to the bed.

That's all my mother can recall of the story. Obviously, my grandfather eventually awakened from his comatose state. No one could have foretold that he would have a special child later in his life—my mother, who was never able to come to the fullest realization of her gifts, even to this day.

The spiritual pattern that afflicted my grandfather was passed on to my mother, and eventually to me. I don't know all the genealogical history in my family, but I'm sure this spiritual pattern began before my grandfather was born.

You have noticed that every-thing an Indian does is in a circle, and that is because the Power of the World always works in circles, and everything tries to be round.

—Black Elk

When my mother was a young girl, she too went into a coma-like state and was actually being prepared for burial rituals when she awoke. She apparently had been "dead" for a number of hours. The local doctor could not get a heartbeat from her, and no one knew what had occurred. She says that when she awoke she was surrounded by faces staring at her, initially in horror at her resurrection. Then there was joy. Later on, they theorized that she might have had some sort of anaphylactic reaction to shellfish she'd consumed. But my mom has continued to gorge on shellfish all her life, without the slightest hesitation or consequence. She is indeed special, a chosen one of the gods and spirits. She still says that she thought she was dreaming every time the Holy Mother appeared at the foot of her bed, yet she traversed the streets of her town praying litanies to her. She never knew how she came to know the words of those prayers, but people would follow her and join in.

In my case, after a number of days in the intensive care unit, I was transferred to a regular bed at New York Hospital. There, I recovered slowly—the prescribed antibiotics still a futile strategy as far as I was concerned. When I left the hospital, I knew I was different. I couldn't explain it then, as an eight-year-old, but I can explain it as I look back now. It is simple: I was no longer a child of this world only. I had been initiated into what would become an intense, intriguing, beguiling, and very challenging spiritual path for years to come.

The miasm had been passed to me not as a burden, but as an opportunity to heal the ancestral imbalances, if you will, of the generations before me. I guess God knew what he was doing, but I could never have imagined the life I was about to live.

My Shaman

Years later, the fragmented pieces of my spiritual path began to make sense...especially after I befriended a 2,000-year-old shaman in the spirit world who would later come to guide and protect me.

One day when I was in my late twenties, I was walking the streets of New York, my physical body visible to the naked eye but my spirit lurking between the worlds. I was praying for someone to help me in the midst of my healing crisis. With my shoulders hunched against the rain-drenched air, I walked slowly, asking the spirits for a healer, for a magician imbued in the teachings of white magic. I needed a herbalist, a dreamer, a spiritwalker. Carrying my medicine bag and gifts for the one I knew must appear, I meandered impatiently and hopefully, trusting that the spirits would soon send someone to assist me.

Despite my years of training in the healing arts, my studies in various spiritual traditions, my training in shamanic work, and my abilities as a medium, I had nothing but my faith to go on in asking for this help. The miasm was beginning to heal on a different level, and I needed a way to move beyond it.

I was shielding my face from a cool drizzle that felt more like ice crystals when I heard small footsteps behind me. I knew they were coming from the spirit world. I stopped, held my breath, and waited to hear the footsteps again. There was silence. I waited another moment before I began to walk again ... and there they were: tiny, mysterious, yet effulgent footsteps. Then a bright light began to emanate as an indomitable soul came forth: a shaman.

He looked at me quizzically, and through telepathic means let me know that he followed the traditions of his grandfathers. That meant that speaking to women was somehow inappropriate, but because of all the work I had done on behalf of the spirit world in the past, he deemed my "call" worthy enough to be answered. (As a medium, I expect spirits simply to talk to me or give me visions—this was the first time a spirit used telepathy to relay his intentions.) He let me know that he was fully aware of why I was there; I didn't need to repeat myself. I was so in awe of his impeccable demeanor, and of a discipline I knew I could never harness, that I was trying not to laugh. He continued our "conversation" telepathically, letting me know that he would help, and showing me how things were beginning to come full circle.

In seeking wisdom, the first state is silence, the second listening, the third remembrance, the fourth practicing, the fifth teaching.
—Rabbi Solomon Ibn Gabirol

Our conversation seemed to last for hours, yet in this earthen reality it was only minutes. He knew of my work as a medium and healer, and was seemingly pleased about my work with plant medicine. After all, he was trained as a shaman in the ritual use of plant spirit medicine. As a spiritwalker, he continues to utilize these gifts, imparting them to those of us in this earthen reality and also to his fellow brethren in the ethers. As we talked, he was accessing my memories on a soul level, letting me know through clairvoyant and clairsentient means what he was seeing … pictures of my childhood, of my initiations, of all the souls who stayed near me from beyond, and of the many remedies that had been given to me over the years to help me heal myself and those who came to me. The plethora of remedies and natural healing cures I had always used in my work came from souls like this shaman. I like to think of these souls as the plant gods.

The plant gods are the teachers and medicine healers of the plants. They have numerous responsibilities. They can summon plant spirits, or plant elementals (fairies, elves, devas, gnomes, and other spirits of nature) at will. They perform plant magic, encourage the relationship between humans and elementals, and facilitate great depths of spiritual healing within and between the worlds. The plant gods are travelers, and exist anywhere in the time and space continuum where souls reside. They are granted certain privileges to heal karma and to work with negativity. They act as a conduit between altered states of reality—this is what enables humans to work with the elementals surrounding the plants. My shaman is himself a plant god, and he came to help me. To this day he has never given me his name, and he still does not communicate with me verbally, only through telepathic means.

As far as plant elementals go, the main thing to remember is that a different elemental will come to each person who works with prayer and plant magic. And a different elemental will come to each plant god who invokes it. Each elemental will have a different teaching on how to best utilize the healing properties of the plant medicine, and the way in which one elemental connects with the plant will be different from how another connects. Likewise, how a human being receives, interprets, and utilizes plant magic will vary from person to person. The manner in which a plant god allocates higher meaning and the vibrational connection between a human and an elemental is up to that plant god.

That cold rainy day was the first time I stood in the presence of my shaman, that sentient being, as he held me in his magic. My body was somewhat erect as I felt his "words" penetrate me. My spirit, weak and sullen, was somehow made stronger by the energies this plant god imparted. The dreamlike state I was in was surreal, even more so because I was utterly exhausted from the spiritual work I had been doing lately. The city block where I encountered the shaman was lined with magnificent pine trees, and I could feel him invoking the trees as he worked with me, calling upon the elementals that he felt could bring me healing. They listened, and they came without hesitation. It was as though the leaves and branches positioned themselves in my direction to protect me, and you could hear the sound of soft whistling in the wind. The air had an etheric feeling and a sense of light pulsation to it, something I am familiar with and attribute to the presence of spirits hovering. He called upon them, one and all, to breathe magic into me and give me hope. It was his prayer, undeniably and exuberantly so.

The shaman's prayer was unspoken, and its vibration traversed every state of consciousness, both tangible and intangible to human senses. Its power was illuminated by the purity of the shaman's intention. And it all happened so fast, as I was passing in and out of some kind of altered state. Something else was unfolding here—a higher level of communication, another level of consciousness and healing.

There is no time boundary when among the spirits, and the hours that passed in my mind lasted only a few minutes in reality. I was in a stupor when the elementals departed.

The shaman, as indomitable as ever, left quietly and walked off into the ethers. He didn't even say goodbye. The gift I had prepared, of stones, hair, and flowers, was now for him, and I sang a song as I looked for a place to lay these intricacies down. I found a home for my offering by one of the trees, and didn't even notice the myriad of people walking to and fro, passing me without observing my bewilderment.

I went home and rested. My meeting with the shaman had been extraordinary. Over the next few months, he returned to show me how my work with the spirit world, specifically with the plant gods, was to release me from the miasm, from the pattern I was born into. This work with plants would also assist me in my efforts to help souls on the other side who are bound to this earth by their own struggles; I would be able to ask the plant spirits for intercession on behalf of souls, and would learn more about the vibrational healing capacities that each living plant embodies, and how that vibration can mirror a thought, emotion, or illness in the earth realm.

But while is easy for me to call upon spirit guides or other souls in the ethers, such is not the case with my shaman. He is a busy soul, and respects the hierarchy of grandfather healers from which he descends. In recent years he has not visited as often as he did during that turbulent and inspiring time when I first met him, but I know where to find him if I have need of him.

In my many years working with clients before I met the shaman, I had received remedies from various healing spirits. These remedies embraced every aspect of human nature, and originated in the plant, mineral, and animal kingdoms. I'd always had a relationship with the spirits who imparted the knowledge. But rarely did I have a relationship with the remedies themselves—and that is what my shaman came to teach me. He wanted me to develop a more personal relationship with the remedies, especially those that came from plants. Meeting the shaman seemed to open a new dimension of the spirit world to me; I now had access to the spirits within this dimension, their healing powers, more remedies than I'd known before, and many new truths about working with plant elementals and spirits of that nature. My awareness was greatly increased, as was my potential to work on another level. For this I am profoundly grateful.

My shaman let me know that, in order to build a more personal relationship with the plant remedies, I needed to be initiated into another dimension of the spirit world and go through a series of healing crises and upheavals. Only after those experiences could I convey my new knowledge. My shaman wanted the new knowledge to heal me, and also wanted me to draw on it to heal others.

Healing Magic

These healing crises and upheavals had already started by the time I met my shaman, which is why I was walking the streets of New York, searching for a soul who could help me. Physically, I was having a severe allergic reaction to pesticides that were being sprayed in my area for mosquitoes, and spiritually, I had been working with the souls of some children who were somehow stuck in the ethers, more or less earthbound and not knowing how to be released into the light.

Every summer, for the past several years, spray trucks had ventured into my neighborhood to kill mosquito larvae. The pesticides were sprayed with little concern for human health and well-being or the environmental devastation they caused, and with little or no advance warning. The first year that the government sprayed, a strong neurotoxin was used that affected many people. My immune system couldn't take the harsh chemicals that seeped through my nervous system, and I was sick for months. The second year, they changed the pesticide, but it still left me debilitated and working hard to clear my body of the harmful residue. By the third year, I thought that I might have built up a resistance to it, but I hadn't. A month after they sprayed, I developed seizure-type episodes. I spent months trying to repattern my nervous and immune systems and hours receiving acupuncture treatments and cranial sacral work. My nutrition focused on increasing essential fatty acids in my diet and any other brain foods I could think of. I also worked with herbs and homeopathy to cleanse out my liver.

Throughout this time, I knew that my work with the lost children in the spirit world also had something to do with my physical condition. I knew that my prayers had to be strong, both for myself and for those whom I was asked to help. Although I had some sort of plan, holistically speaking, it still felt like I was chasing my tail. Something was missing—so I sat down one day and came up with a new strategy. I needed to invoke the spirit world as only I knew how, and ask what they needed from me to help me move beyond my malady. I also wanted them to teach me how to work with the toxins in my body on a different level.

Crazy Horse dreamed and went into the world where there is nothing but the spirits of all things. That is the real world that is behind this one, and everything we see here is something like a shadow from that world.
—Black Elk

A major part of this new plan was meeting a spirit who would come and assist me. I knew I would have to go through a metamorphosis, and I balked at the idea of having to endure some of the trials I knew would come, but I had no choice. I was stuck. My body wasn't able to rebalance and rid itself of the pesticide residue, and the lost children were constantly around me, sometimes playing, sometimes crying, attaching themselves to me to such a degree that other clairvoyant mediums could see them around me. Their energies were very heavy, since they were frightened, and their souls were very old. I was stuck, they were stuck, and we were going nowhere together.

After I met my shaman, I could always tell when he was present, since the vibration and energy in the air around me would shift. The light would deepen and the walls would look like shadows in a multidimensioned structure that enclosed me. I always waited patiently for his visits and little by little, he imparted instruction and healing—my initiation into the work with plants had begun. I was addled by his methodology, but it didn't matter; I needed his help, and took down some notes. I was still bewildered as to how the lost children could help my physical body convalesce, and how the plant magic would play into all of this.

To explain my relationship with the lost children, I should first share some of my own spiritual practices. When I pray in the morning, I always pray for the souls in purgatory and in other dimensions of the spirit world. I was raised Catholic and revere the teachings of the Christian saints and martyrs, especially when it comes to the repose of a soul. I also embrace the Buddhist teachings of reincarnation, and have somehow intertwined the two so that they fit my understanding and development. Many times during prayer and in my state of contemplation, souls come and go around me, asking for me to pray for them. Simple enough. As a Catholic, I draw from the many wonderful prayers that have been passed down through the ages, especially prayers for souls who are not at rest. I also devote time to creating my own sacred words for the heavens.

One memorable day, I was saying a prayer to St. Joseph to benefit children, specifically the ones who had been coming to me. One by one, they entered the living room where I sat silently, and began to laugh and move in concentric circles around me. They made me laugh, and I tried not to pay too much attention to them as they watched me. I wasn't sure why I was even praying for them, since they seemed so happy. New children always came each day, and some of the ones who had visited me previously would return. I usually would laugh with them for a moment, then return to my novenas.

But on this day, my curiosity got the better of me and I sat with them for a while, wondering where they had come from and why they were there. One of them took me through the spirit world to an orphanage in Europe during the late 1800s or early 1900s, and showed me that some of the children who had been visiting me had died there of the plague. The care they received was dismal, and most of them longed for companionship. Their clothes were thin and tattered, their stomachs distended from starvation, and their teeth rotting from malnutrition. They came to me "happy" because they lived each day in the orphanage in a state of make-believe. They pretended to be joyful and carefree, with warm meals filling their tummies and shoes with laces that were as strong as steel, ones that wouldn't break during their free-spirited play. They played both by themselves and with one another, but often were sickly. They mostly stayed inside the orphanage, looking through the dirt-stained windows to get a glimpse of the outside world.

There were other children who visited me as well, from various places and times in earthen reality. The common thread seemed to be that they had all been abandoned in some manner. Some had been abused, many had lived on the streets, and many died from disease. All in all, I got to "meet" them and hear their stories.

But how were these children connected to my physical condition, and how was the shaman going to help me? How was I going to learn what he wanted me to learn about his work with plant medicine? It all seemed overwhelming to me, but as the children kept coming and staying near, my body would feel their illnesses, and their emotions would run through me. There were days I was stronger and days I was weaker. I continued to do the same self-care things I'd always done, while awaiting the next steps from my new spirit friend.

The shaman came every so often at the beginning, bringing me healing energy. He would use his prayers and plant magic. The first time he asked me to lie down on my living room floor, so that he could do some healing work on me, was memorable. As he came near, other souls began to come out of the ethers and gather with him around me. He called upon them, and then, with his prayers, he called upon the plants. He summoned one plant in particular: *Phytolacca americana*. Poke.

May all things move and be moved in me and know and be known in me. May all creation dance for joy within me.
—Chinook Psalter

The spirits and souls around me were preparing the plant for me. It is a miraculous thing to behold spirits bringing you healing. Although I wasn't able to see the plant elementals who were present, I could perceive them through clairaudience and clairsentience, and the spirits and souls around me all seemed to be aware of the elementals springing forth. Their relationship with the elementals was one of beneficence and complete trust. I then understood that these spirits and souls were plant gods. And the elementals—the spirits of many different plants—were their joyful cohorts.

The shaman wanted to show me one of the lifetimes where this miasm of mine began. I was one of them, a medicine woman in the Native American tradition. I was suffering from what looked like a bout of tuberculosis. A healer was making an herbal preparation for me, and I went through a cathartic healing crisis before I became well. It looked like they'd called upon the poke plant back then, as well. There were children around me in that lifetime, playing. Some of them had stayed with me; their lightheartedness was what had attracted some of the lost children who also were now at my side. Apparently I'd never let them go. Then the vision of myself in that lifetime dissipated, and I continued to stay present with the healing that the spirits were facilitating for me.

The spiritual energies of the poke plant were like an aphrodisiac. The spirits seemed to dance around me with the preparation that they made, and their laughter was so voluminous that I couldn't contain myself, and joined in. I could tell that they were releasing some kind of held energy within me, physically, emotionally, and spiritually. My laughter turned into coughing and a metallic taste formed on the tip of my tongue. I knew that I was ridding some of that pesticide residue from my system. My coughing went deeper, until I was able to push up some mucus, and then it subsided. There was an emptiness within and around me. Something had given way in my chest, and all I could feel was the emptiness.

My past life as a medicine woman no longer seemed to hold any energy in my energy field, and I knew that some of the lost children had made their way into the light. It was only a handful, but it was a start. I felt empty, even sad, and I realized how tightly I was holding onto souls that I didn't even know were attaching to me so strongly. I'd probably been doing this since the day I was born. I wondered whether, if my thinking had not been so myopic, I could have helped these children into the light any earlier, through prayer.

Our life too is threefold. In the first stage we have our being, in the second our growth, and in the third our perfection.
—Julian of Norwich

I guess it didn't matter. The timing was right, and perhaps there was more meaning then I realized in their attachment to me. As I lifted myself up, the shaman was still around me, but the other souls had vanished. The etheric mist that accompanies the spirit world was very profuse. I could breath better—I could definitely feel that—and something had shifted for me physically. Later, when I looked at myself in the mirror, I saw that my coloring was not as yellow as it had been ever since the spraying of the pesticides began. I had many questions, but the shaman wasn't about to give me many answers. This was going to be a memorable relationship and apprenticeship.

When those few of the lost children crossed into the light, they had taken some of the poison out of my body so that I could really begin to heal. And some of the internal inflammation that I had tried to calm through other means had shifted slightly. Even my eyesight was a little better, for a while. I knew that there had to be reasons why the children had been with me for all those years, but it didn't really matter. Now just seemed to be the time to start healing this miasm. The teacher had appeared, and the work had begun.

I did want to know more about the poke plant that day, since it was obviously very strengthening for me. When I asked the shaman about it, he prayed, as though getting permission from a higher source to impart the knowledge. He then began to show me some of its healing properties. He didn't call upon the elementals again to dictate the plant magic; rather, he simply funneled it in a way that I could see it for myself. He was trying to teach me not just about connecting to the plant elementals, but also about connecting with the gods who have dominion over them.

When the shaman invoked poke, his lips formed subtle syllables as he raised his head toward the sky. I could hear only what appeared to be mumbling... perhaps a song, a prayer. He sang what came to him; he sang what came through him. I felt the energy come down through my crown chakra, into my heart, and ground through the earth. His prayer was as melodious a chant as I have ever heard. Even though its words would seem inane, if even audible, to a normal person, they made sense to me because of their vibration.

He let me see for a brief moment into the window of his world, of his spiritual makeup, of his gifting from the One Creator. And I saw poke through his eyes. Tears started to roll down my cheeks as my own prayer began to form, words like butterflies flying effortlessly from my lips to God's ears:

> *"Great Creator and Spirit of the Buffalo, we surrender to your powerful medicine. We stand here before you, seeking guidance and direction. Bring to us your wisdom, Great Spirit, so that we may follow in the trails you leave behind. Show us the way, for we are your children."*

I was hearing the words in my head, and the melody was ringing in my voice. Wow—that was my prayer. When my spirit reached out to the soul of the poke plant, the prayer just began to emanate from my lips. The joy I felt in this sacred communion was illuminating. The emptiness I'd felt just a few moments before, after the healing, was now filled. My heart and soul felt whole. I had released something back to spirit—some of the children—and it felt like this connection, this joy, was their gift to me in return.

The soul is an empty vessel, but the Creator looks at emptiness much differently than we do. There is great splendor in finding union, and great ecstasy in creating a relationship with the higher power. All things stem from the Creator, and all unions are meant to be made in the image and likeness of our union with the Creator. There is emptiness as we search aimlessly for this connection, and there is utter bliss when we find it.

In my prayer to poke, I had found that bliss for a moment. I looked at my shaman, and gratitude filled my heart for his kindness toward me. Before he left the room, he helped me to see some of poke's healing qualities. Later, I would learn more about this plant from the elemental that came to me. At the moment, however, I was receiving transmissions of energy directly from the plant god—my shaman—and knowledge about poke directly from him. Here are some of the images and wisdom I received for poke:

From an aboriginal point of view, no one can accomplish anything who is not in alignment with the gods or a God.
—Malidoma Some

> *… This amazing creation of nature can bring warmth and love to one's heart. It can alleviate fear and anxiety and help promote a deep sense of faith and trust in self and in one's spiritual path. Poke heals broken spirits throughout all creation. It is a plant of enormous strength and is used for protection. It can induce trance-like states of consciousness for purposes of healing.*

There was more; there was much more. I knew these healing messages were meant for me, but I felt that others would benefit from them as well.

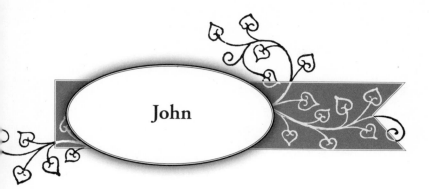

John

After the shaman left, I knew I had some work to do. One of the first instructions he'd given me, during our previous conversations, was about helping a male soul who was unable to cross into the light. Since I was receiving help myself, it was my obligation to help others. I had listened to the shaman, not really knowing the direction I was headed and not sure what he had in mind. But I had faith in him.

When he asked me to visit the local cemetery, I thought he was crazy. I don't especially like cemeteries, since earthbound souls sometimes linger there. But the next day I got in my car and drove for about five minutes. The cemetery is one of the largest in this part of New York City, and I didn't have a clue where to go. I prayed, and then was guided to drive down a narrow street and park my car near the cemetery gates that were open. I figured that the shaman would meet me there.

I got out of my car and hesitantly walked through the aisles of gravestones. I took with me my rosary, a candle, my prayer books, and some gifts of flowers. I looked around to make sure the caretaker or another employee of the cemetery was nowhere near—I was afraid if they saw me with all those trinkets, I would get kicked out. As I was walking, I called upon the shaman and asked him to show me where I was supposed to go. I glanced at the hundreds of headstones until my eyes came upon what looked like a portal of light. Below the portal was a small and very antiquated headstone, next to a glorious tree. I looked around, just to make sure I wasn't seeing things or that the light wasn't above any other headstone.

All are but parts of one stupendous whole,
Whose body Nature is,
And God the soul; ...
Look around our World;
Behold the chain of Love
Combining all below and all above.
—Alexander Pope

I waited a few moments, then walked over to the grave site and lay my tools on the ground. I sat under the tree. It was autumn and the ground was a little cold and bare. I felt uneasy and began to question everything. Did I really need to go this route? I was very glad that the shaman had come into my life, but was the path I was taking going to bring me healing? More importantly, would peace come to those lost children who had embedded themselves in my energy field and, ultimately, in my home? I wasn't sure. And I was tired. I wanted to bargain—I was willing to do the work that was needed to fully heal, but I didn't want to add any more to my plate if it wasn't necessary. I went back and forth with these thoughts for a few minutes, wondering again whether, if I stayed true to my holistic modalities, within time the pesticides would fully clear from my immune and nervous systems. And I wondered if, with unceasing prayer, the lost children would finally come to rest.

I was jolted out of my indecisive musings by a grounds-worker who asked if I was okay. I told him yes, and thanked him for checking up on me. He didn't say anything about the spiritual tools that were on the ground in front of me. I guess he just assumed that I was praying for someone that I'd lost. He went away, and I gave my attention to the headstone surrounded by light. I don't remember the exact inscription. I do, however, remember that the name was John, and that he died in the early 1900s. There wasn't anything remarkable about his headstone; it was actually pretty ordinary, and felt lonesome to me. I wondered who John was and why I was there to help him.

So how do you call upon a soul in the spirit world? I just ask for them. And I tell my clients the same thing—just call spirits by name. Either they will come or, if your prayers are fervent, someone else who can give you messages about them will come. So I called. I called John. My face began to glow with warmth, which usually happens when I open up to the spirit world. I called John, and alternately, I called my plant god, my shaman.

"John, my name is Laura. I'm not sure what I am doing here, but I'm supposed to pray for you. I don't know if you can hear me or even want to hear me; I just want you to know I'm here. I don't mean to bother you, but you feel kind of lonely to me, and I was wondering if there was anything I could do for you." I didn't hear anything. I didn't know if I would hear him, or see him, or both. I took my red-beaded rosebud rosary and began praying the Divine Chaplet, and with that, the Catholic prayers for eternal rest. As I repeated the same prayer with each delicate rosebud bead, the portal seemed to grow bigger and bigger, and the light seemed to emanate in all directions.

I kept going until I began to notice that an energy was present. I was enervated by it. My heart began to pound and become weak, and I became aware that there was some anger and bitterness present. I knew that the presence wasn't my shaman, so it had to be John.

"John, is that you?" I asked. I didn't hear a response, but my body was mirroring his more and more, so I knew I had to hold a stronger boundary. I could also tell that John had been a smoker when he was alive. I repeated myself. "John, are you there?" Still, no one answered. I could tell he was frightened; I could tell he was lost. I could feel that he didn't trust anybody. Sometimes this happens with a spirit when a medium is trying to make a connection. The soul may not want to speak up, or it may take a while for them to trust you, especially if they have been wandering the earth as a lost soul for years. When this happens, it has been my experience that other souls who are very aware of this soul will intercede on their behalf and do the communicating.

I felt it was him, and that he was observing my every move from beyond the veil. I called to my shaman for help, and to any other spirits who could give me a little more insight into John's earthbound reality. And boy, did they come. A number of John's family members came, who had not been able to reach John before. They had been looking for him, but for some reason could not find him. They had been waiting a long time to be reunited with him. Through these spirits, I got to see a little of John's life. He seemed to be a midshipman, a sailor, I think for the navy. He lost the love of his life early on, and stayed alone for the rest of his years. He didn't really spend much time associating or socializing with others, but mostly kept to himself. He seemed to be a handsome man—tall, with light eyes and hair strewn across his head. This information was not coming to me from John but from those who loved him most, as well as from my spirit guides. John's gravestone looked untouched and inviolable, as though it had not been visited or disturbed in years.

Melancholy came over me as I tried to reach out to John directly, but it was of no avail. I kept praying, and turned my vision to the shaman. I asked him to intercede and help John, or in the very least show me how to help him. The shaman asked me to be patient with John. While the methods I am accustomed to were helping, they didn't seem to be enough, which is why I thought my plant god might have another way.

There is always more than one way to help a soul who is stuck. There are many spiritual traditions that offer rites of passage and ceremonial tributes to the dearly departed. There are also thousands of prayers devoted to the dead. My shaman's way of helping souls is simply one of these many approaches—one which I was going to learn.

I looked at my shaman intently. My eyes were dazzled by the gleaming sunlight that seemed to land right in front of my feet, near the headstone. I waited, and he watched. Then he took his staff and lifted it up to the sky, as though embracing the omnipotence of the spirits of nature. In my psychic vision, his brown skin radiated with gentleness and such utter faith that the sight left me motionless. I don't even remember taking a breath. He began to mumble, like he had done before; unrecognizable syllables emanated from his lips. He was one with his words, and his eyes were lowered in reverence, even though his head was tilted toward the sunlight.

He was saying his prayer, invoking the plant spirits. I wasn't privileged to see which of the elementals he was invoking; my attention was focused on the sweet melody that reverberated with each breath he took. It went on and on, and it was glorious. I glanced at the tree above me and I could swear that the leaves were dancing to his prayer. They were smiling to his song. There were still some green leaves left, even though autumn hues graced the entirety of the tree. And they were luminous—every red, auburn, burnt-orange, green, pointed, withered leaf. Luminous, every one of them. And they knew they were being summoned.

When a plant spirit is summoned, all of nature listens, and many elementals will adhere to the call, even if just for support. So when one is called, all embark. The responsibility may be left to only one elemental, or it can be left to many; that is the decision of the plant god. Thus, the trees glistened, the sun shone even brighter, the clouds above formed what looked like celestial shapes, and the birds came nearer to where I sat. Others could only see a woman, with her rosary and some religious oddities, sitting on the ground by a headstone. But to me, I was in the presence of greatness—a sea of spiritual beings and souls who wanted to serve. I was in awe.

Even the headstones in the cemetery seemed to awaken; or rather, the souls attached to them awakened. I felt blissful. The souls around John started to pay attention to the song, and eventually, so did John. They didn't see the shaman; they did see me, though. And they responded to his prayer to the plant spirits. They clasped their hands in the hopes that this prayer would reach John in some way. I saw John looking for the source of this heavenly inspiration. I could feel him look my way to see if I was singing this prayer, and I obviously could not take the credit. When I saw that he was responding, I continued praying with my rosary so that John could receive all the help that he needed.

His energy started to brighten as his curiosity grew. Where was this sacred sound coming from? The vibrations were so strong that it seemed to open a portal, so that John could see the family members that were waiting for him. He looked at them. His shoulders loosened, as did his protective stance. His chest muscles seemed to relax in a way that they hadn't in lifetimes. He looked up and gazed at what I believe was light. The gloominess and shadowing that had marked his facial features seemed to lift.

My heart lightened, as though my own burdens were dissipating. It was as if I were in the midst of a family reunion that was hundreds of years overdue. John's demeanor changed dramatically, and the overtones in the air seemed to quell any anxieties that John had about my disturbing him. My shaman continued to sing his prayer, and tears welled up in my eyes. I had totally forgotten that I was sitting in the middle of New York City, in one of the largest cemeteries in the county, on an autumn day, under a tree, in a front of a headstone of a man I had never known.

Hold onto what is good, even if it is a handful of earth. Hold onto what you believe, even if it is a tree which stands by itself. Hold onto what you must do, even if it is a long way from here. Hold onto life, even if it is easier to let go. Hold onto my hand, even when I have gone away from you.
—Pueblo Blessing

The air started to clear, and as quickly as John and his relatives came, they made their way together into the next dimension—the light that was awaiting them. My shaman stayed, and the other helping spirits who supported us departed. It is not uncommon for me to feel a great emptiness when I come out of such a high vibration of souls and spirits, to rest gently in the arms of earthen reality. That emptiness was present now, even though one soul was left, and he was still praying.

I asked the shaman if it was appropriate for him to tell me which plant elemental he'd called upon, specifically, to help John in his crisis. Like last time, I waited. And then I started to hum. It felt like my heart strings were being tickled, and I hummed even louder. Then from my lips, a prayer to lemon balm came, and with it, the elemental—who wanted to show herself to me.

"Fly, little fairy, as fast as you can, and bring magic to each lemon balm with the stroke of your

hand. Using your wand, filled with God's grace, make nectar of its leaves for the entire human race."

I repeated the prayer as quickly as it came, over and over again, my head spinning with dizziness at the burst of energy that accompanied the prayer. As I spoke, a little effervescent fairy came whizzing by. She was delicate but strong, and in her tiny hand she carried a wand of magic. She alighted upon each leaf of the lemon balm plant in the spirit world, and tapped her wand to activate the healing magic of the plant.

She told me she would come to me again at a later time to share more of her magic and how she imparts it to help humans, but she wanted to share with me now some of the healing qualities that her magic brings to people.

She let me know that lemon balm is the plant of gathering for spiritual communion. My shaman had called upon her and, by virtue of his power, was able to intensify and bridge the karmic connections that exist between the plant kingdom and the human world. She heeded my shaman's call and came into the energy sphere with John and his family members, and helped to open the portal that healed the rift. The fairy helped John overcome his fear of being in the world, both the one he'd lived his last existence in and the dimension he resided in now. She brought him courage, and helped to soothe his soul and the grief he'd carried for years. She brought immediate comfort to his heartache and helped put his wandering mind at ease.

With his heart healed, he was able to be free.

I was tired. I left the cemetery, feeling much more peaceful than when I'd arrived, and went home.

A Karmic
Healing Response

Over the next few days, I went into yet another healing crisis. My skin turned a pale yellowish color, my hair became brittle again, and my skin seemed more taut. I went to bed each night with my body burning as though I had been through a chemical reaction. I was sweating, and my face would swell. My body would shake as if I had the chills, but internally, I always felt feverish. I would lie there in bed until some of the symptoms subsided. It was always the worst at night time.

During the day, I was mindful of my diet and the supplements I was taking. I would eat, lightly, foods that would continue to cleanse my liver and gallbladder. I spent time doing castor oil packs and taking salt and baking soda baths. Herbal plant baths were also part of my agenda. Whatever I needed to do to get through this healing crisis, I would do it.

In response to my prayers, the spirits assured me that I was just detoxing from the poisons in my body. They even let me know beforehand what would occur, to lessen any

fear that I might have. I have always trusted in these helping spirits, who relay healing information to me. They have
dictated information that I have shared with my clients over
the years.

*I have seen that in any great
undertaking it is not enough
for a man to depend simply
upon himself.*
—Lone Man, Teton Sioux

During this time, I often looked at an
angel statue my sister had given me one Christmas, and whenever I psychically saw her face
swell up or her eyes get red, I knew that this
would happen to me as well. It is common-
place for objects belonging to a person to take
on their energy, which is why psychics can look
at someone's picture or hold a piece of clothing and tell a lot
about a person. My home and the things in it have taken on
my energy, so it is easy for me to see what might be going
on within myself if I look at my possessions. And it wasn't
just the angel statue that confirmed what was happening to
me—all of the statuary in my home told me things about my
health. I used these psychic visions as confirmation of what I
heard from the spirits in my prayers.

Also, during such healing crises, I found myself under
spiritual duress, torment, and attack. I was more open and
vulnerable, because my body was so weak and my boundaries were permeable. I spent a lot of time at my local cha-
pel whenever this occurred, and much time doing protection rituals. I needed to pray often, and spiritual cleansing
became my ordinary reality. When I was this sensitive, I
would stay clear of large groups of people or busy places,
anything that held frenetic energy. I just knew it wouldn't be
good to put myself in a position of taking on more energy. I
would also distance myself from people or places that held a
lot of negative energy, and those places where a lot of souls
tended to gather and wander. It is part of the work, and part
of what I need to do to respect the nature of who I am and
the gifts that were given to me.

And during those healing crises, I was lucky to have support from friends, colleagues, and teachers. One such source of support was Ida. She is the most gregarious, fiery, and opinionated seer I have ever known. I met Ida through one of my own clients, and she was a part of my family from that very first meeting. Ida is her own anomaly, unique and undefined. She is a seer through the ancient art of tasseography: she reads coffee grinds, as did her mother before her. What stands out is that Ida will not allow anyone in her home to have their grinds read. You need to have a car, so that your grinds may be read as you are parked in the vicinity with Ida at your side. She is forthright. As a client, you pick her up at the appointed time and drive a few blocks away to a location where you both feel comfortable. Then this elder seer takes out her blue rectangular tray, a large white plate to disseminate the coffee grinds on, and a little jar of water for washing the grinds away when she needs to see new formations on the plate. Ida is an experience for everyone to try. She loves spirits, particularly leprechauns, and the plant spirits love her. I can tell, because each time we walk past flowering plants, they seem to bend her way.

During my current healing crisis, I knew I needed someone—physical, in the earth plane—to help me. The work I had done in the cemetery had helped bring clarity to the souls involved, but also, since it cleared an energetic pattern in my own healing process, it had caused physical upheaval in my body. I needed Ida.

I made my way over to Queens on a bright autumn day to seek her assistance. We walked to my car; I carried her cornucopia of grounds-reading tools. She settled herself into my "talking car," as she always liked to call it. (She nicknamed it this because every time she said something the spirits approved of, the car alarm would beep.)

Our favorite parking space was in a lot behind a local drugstore and our favorite pizzeria; we would pull in there and find a spot away from the other cars. Ida poured the Turkish coffee into the espresso coffee cup and I drank a little, since Ida wanted some of the coffee along with the grinds for the reading. If you have ever tried Turkish coffee, you know that it has a very dark and bitter taste—it's an acquired taste, at that.

Ida looked at the cup. She said there was a man standing there, a medicine man, a healer. She described him as having brown skin and a magic staff. I knew immediately that it was my shaman. She said that he was helping me and not to worry, for he was a good soul. She also saw that I was not feeling too well. She said that it was from a poison in my body, a poison that was trying to make its way out, slowly but surely.

She also saw negative spirits that were pestering me during the night. She told me not to worry, that they bother me because I'm a good soul and they would rather not see me get better. Whenever Ida sees souls like this, she takes her jar of water and just washes them away. But before she did that, a big cross appeared in one of the plates, visible even to my untrained eye. Ida looked at me and said that God was with me, so I should try and worry less.

We talked about a lot of other things that were helpful that day. Once in while a remedy would appear on the plate, or something about eating the right food or about some emotional upset I was focused on. Whatever it was, Ida brought healing to it. And just as it was with my shaman, I felt so much better when I left her presence.

As winter drew near and the cold humid weather seemed to project its tendrils into the city, I focused on the work I had learned with my shaman. My body was getting a little stronger each day, and I anxiously waited for the next piece of the puzzle to work with and integrate. The lost children continued to come. Even though some had crossed over, there were still what felt like hundreds stuck somewhere in the spirit world. I prayed for them daily, recounting the healings that the shaman and his helpers facilitated for me. Prayers and novenas to various Catholic saints would echo from my lips, and the children would continue to scatter about me and play with me from beyond the veil. Some of them really did not want to leave my company—and for that matter, I didn't want to lose theirs. Even so, I intuitively knew that one by one, they would someday go home, fully home.

The daylight grew shorter, and the holidays came upon us. I decided to enjoy some of the festivities and took a trip to the local zoo to see the Christmas lights. It was cold that night, and the sight of the illumined faces of children grasping their parents' hands was exhilarating. I felt like a child again. Whether we were forty years old or seven, we all looked with wonder at the lighted displays of Christmas magic. The petting zoo was open as well, and I enjoyed myself along with the kids, petting the farm animals. The night wouldn't have been complete without a hot pretzel, of course. It is rare for me to eat one, but I did so that night with joyous gluttony.

As I took my last bite of that salted, floury treat, I thought I saw my shaman out of the corner of my eye. I did a double take, and when he was nowhere to be found I thought it was my imagination. Over the past few weeks I'd talked to him occasionally, but he seemed busy, and I knew that when the time was right he would reappear.

If only you could suddenly be unaware of all things, then you could pass into an oblivion of your own body.
—Meister Eckhart

I walked toward the petting zoo again, and watched the children climb up on the fences to touch whichever animal came closest to them. Their anticipation was overwhelming.

I could feel how special it felt to be chosen by one of the animals, as the one whom the animal chose to commune with. After an animal made its choice, the other children would run over to the child who was "picked" to see if they could pet the animal too. This went on all night long. I even think the lost children followed me, because I could hear them laughing and giggling from the other side. They wanted to enjoy a bit of Christmas magic, too.

Many of the talents and abilities we have been reserving for 'higher' animals may in fact be part of the experience of all living things. In our attempts to understand the origin and nature of awareness, we ought to be looking far more closely, and more literally to our roots.

—Lyall Watson

I finally left the petting zoo area and began walking down a narrow path that led to the camel exhibit. As I stopped by some flora that draped the pathway, I heard footsteps behind me, coming from the spirit world. They were gentle footsteps, watching me and protecting me. I knew the shaman was there. I'd had a few weeks to rest after our work with John and his relatives at the cemetery; my physical body needed that time to integrate, cleanse, and heal. My shaman was ready to continue the work, and I trusted that he knew I was ready, too.

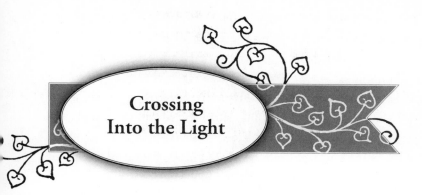

Crossing Into the Light

The next day, in the midst of seeing clients, I knew with certainty that the shaman would soon come to show me the next piece of the puzzle. When he arrived later, he told me to go to the home of an acquaintance and do some spiritual cleansing there. Since I wasn't used to going into homes and cleansing them, I was a little hesitant about what my goal would be there.

The shaman explained that when I went into the home, I would see where some of the lost children came from. Years ago, the house had known abuse—spiritual, emotional, and mental. There had been four children living there, and all of them were very open to the spirit world. For some reason, the lost children who now surrounded me had attached themselves to them, as I'm sure they attached themselves to children all over the world who had similar spiritual patterns. I can't address the needs of the entire world, obviously, but it has always been my belief that when you help one, you help hundreds. When you help hundreds, you heal thousands. And when you heal thousands, a miracle happens. So numbers don't matter, because the efficacy of prayer moves mountains.

Before going to the house, I called my acquaintance (who knew a little about my work) and simply explained that I believed there were some stuck souls in his home; could I come in and pray? I told him that I thought it would help his health, as well. He was unbelievably fine with this proposal. I then went and bought some vanilla wafer cookies for the children, and some flowers. I also found a teddy bear I'd had since childhood.

The next day, when I walked into the house, I saw that it hadn't been cleaned in years. The walls were dilapidated and dirt hung from every corner—I almost walked out due to the scent of decay in there. It was sparsely furnished. I made my way through the house and into the smaller bedrooms. The girls used to sleep in one bedroom and their brother in another. Old posters and books were strewn across the floor and walls. I just looked around in disbelief for a while.

Finally, I took one of the chairs and lay the flowers on it. I got a bowl for the cookies and put some of the vanilla wafers in it. The teddy bear looked perfect sitting between the cookies and the flowers. As I walked through the house again, I called my shaman, and also kept talking to the lost children who had once lived there, letting them know that I was in a home they would probably recognize on some level. They wouldn't actually recognize the house as one they had occupied, but on a psychic level, they might perceive that it was a manifestation of an energy matrix they already knew, a physically manifested metaphor.

Everything on the earth has a purpose, every disease an herb to cure it, and every person a mission. This is the Indian theory of existence.
—Mourning Dove Salish

In the living room, I felt a portal between an old velvet-covered chair and a twenty-year-old TV set. What felt like a gust of wind went through me; opening my psychic vision wider, I could indeed see a wondrous portal awaiting the children. I was elated at the possibility of some continued healing for them. I went back into the bedroom and began to pray, knowing my shaman would be present when I needed him. I began with my rosary, and then with the novenas that have always worked. I talked to the children in between the prayers. This was going to take more than one day—it would take a number of days and I would have to come back to this home often. I remember looking at the ceiling and saying to myself that the ceiling would collapse after the work was done.

I felt a presence behind me, which I assumed was my shaman. I turned around, and to my surprise it was John, the soul from the cemetery. He wanted to help in some way, and I began to truly understand how all things and souls connect. For some reason, it was his karma to help in the work. It didn't matter how; even just bringing me reassurance and extra protection was enough. I smiled and then continued praying. John was a humble and sweet presence, very different from the soul I'd originally encountered at the cemetery.

The energy and temperature in the room became frigid and I could vividly see the moisture in my breath. My body temperature also dropped and my extremities became ice-cold. The children became quiet for a while. I fervently repeated every word of every prayer, with the hopes that some of the children would see the portal and cross.

John stayed with me and when the time was right, my shaman appeared. The lost children still remained quiet—no laughing, no playing, no hide-and-seek. I comforted myself against the coldness of the air and felt some unusual presences.

The orange-colored room was starting to feel more like a prison, and visions began coming to me of children from long ago. It seemed that many more lost children lived in this house than the four I'd been looking for. And these were visions I had not seen before—the energies startled me. These children were horrified; many of them had gone through some sort of ritualistic abuse. I also saw trains, many trains, and saw what looked like uniforms belonging to concentration camps. The energy of the abuse began to feel cultish in nature to me. I had a sense that some of the children in my visions were headed off to the concentration camps we read about in history books. Some of them had been kidnapped and suffered much. They all died in horror, some with chemical poisoning, others from starvation. I was petrified to be "seeing" all of this, and really thought it couldn't be true. I felt a hand on my shoulder at one point—John, letting me know he was there with me.

I took a deep breath and wondered how it related to me, if at all. Then an idea dawned on me. The miasm—these souls must have been around my mom, and assumably around my grandfather as well. Who knows how long they had been in my family's energy matrix. Both my mom and my grandfather had had those strange, near-death experiences. Since I don't know very much about my family history in the literal sense, I can only surmise that in some way, these children attached themselves to my family during those deathlike trances, and were then passed on to me. The poisoning from the pesticides and what it did to my body had never made clinical sense. Why, for a year, did the skin on my body burn each night as I went to bed, making me writhe in pain between my blankets until it subsided? I could understand that an allergic reaction would cause that kind of sensation, but for so long a time was uncanny. Pieces of my puzzle were finally starting to fit—I was getting at least some understanding into the reasons behind the intensity of my health situation.

As I was integrating these pieces together, my body went into some sort of pain reaction. I continued to pray while figuring everything out. If I could make the connection between myself and these children, then it would be easier for them to cross over and for me to let go. Now that I realized how often they had been around my mother, I guessed that there had to have been a family ancestor who directly experienced some kind of trauma similar to what I was seeing. And in his or her quest to be free, the negativity surrounding that ancestor had taken hold of other family members, propelling them into that deathlike trance state.

There is no death, only a change of worlds.
—Seattle, Suquamish Chief

The children were trying to free themselves, but they just didn't know how. My familial line was familiar to them, so they'd hung around for quite a while hoping someone would notice them. I still wasn't exactly sure why this house was chosen for this moment, or why some of those children's spirits lived there, but I assume it had something to do with what went on with the children who'd lived there. Most likely, the children who lived there fragmented psychologically in some way due to the abuse they'd endured, and in their disconnect, they opened up to other planes of consciousness. I trust that the other young spirits attached to them to bring them some sort of comfort and relief.

There was no pragmatic answer here, but there were bits and pieces that could formulate a synopsis of what had transpired, energetically, over the last few generations in my family. After I left, I talked to the homeowner and got his okay for future visits—the days I'd planned to be there had just extended themselves.

My dreams became more lifelike over the next few days, as I could not escape the horrors that I'd seen and felt with those children's souls. I wasn't sleeping well. Part of that had to do with the fact that these new children were now around me more, and their pain had become mine until they could find solace. Emotionally, physically, and spiritually, we all seemed to be purifying at the same time.

My moods also began to change as I started working with this specific group of children. I isolated myself more and kept very few friends by my side. I talked with my mom often, but pretty much stayed disciplined in embracing the space that I needed to carry myself through this. Physically, my chemical sensitivities increased for a period of time. My sense of smell was so delicate and attuned—I was repelled by the scent of hair spray or perfume. My eyesight was out of focus—my vision would vacillate between nearsightedness and farsightedness. My energy field was so open that being near people became challenging. I was ornery. My appetite was unusual, as were my food cravings. My blood-sugar levels would rise and fall and I was becoming increasingly food-sensitive. And the body burning... every night, like clockwork, it would take its toll. I would clench my jaw so tightly that my mouth would hurt in the morning from grinding my teeth.

I saw my holistic practitioners as often as I could; they reflected on my need for extra protection and continued prayer. I also did a lot of work on my own. But I was getting tired—emotionally, physically, and spiritually. Even though the shaman had come into my life only a short time ago, I'd been working with the lost children for a while before that, and fighting the pesticides in my body at the same time. I felt like I was lingering, suspended in some kind of spiritual anima-tion. My priest had advised that whenever I took on a spiri-tual endeavor, I should always ask God if this is the work I should be doing. Go over and above the minds of the teach-ers in the spirit world, he said, and ask God. Well, I did ask

God, over and over again. The answer was the same all the time.

One evening the body-burning got really bad. The children were waiting for me to go back to the house a second time. A smell of fear and of dead animal carcasses permeated my house that evening. I kept looking at my herbs and my plants. I needed the shaman; I needed my plant god to distill his magic, because I was weak.

I drew a bath and asked the shaman what plants to put in it. I knew he would respond, and even though I couldn't see him this time, I could hear his answer clearly: "Rosemary and rue." I happened to have both of them on hand.

I took a handful of each and held them gingerly. Sometimes I just tossed plants into the bath; other times I steeped them and then poured the plant water in with the bath water. I always prayed with my plants before bathing with them, however, and I wanted my shaman to pray with me, to energize and infuse the plants and the prayers with his magic, his gifts from the Creator.

I offered my prayers for both the rosemary and the rue— but not my usual prayers, because this time, I wanted to sing to the plants' souls, like my shaman did.

I pulled the rosemary toward my heart and begun to sing its song:

> *"O Divine Mother, all loving, all knowing, ever so present. Fill our hearts with the grace of your love. Hold us in your tender arms. Give to us divine mercy in our suffering. Be with us at the time of our loneliness. Show us how to be compassionate with ourselves and with humankind. Teach us the ways of God."*

With that prayer, a little girl plant spirit came out of the ethers. She was transparent in nature, and very connected with the Divine Mother energy. She was filled with pure, unconditional love and had a special relationship with the plant world. She had her own garden in the ethers, and cared for all of her plants, especially rosemary. She was lovely as she whirled around me, psychically placing sprigs of rosemary in my hair. She told me not to worry, that I would be okay. She also said that the lost children would be okay too. She showed me that I would go back to their house soon, and that in the end, they would be fine. I placed the rosemary in my tub and knew that the energies imparted by both the little girl elemental and my shaman would make the bathwater strong.

The little girl danced her way back into the ethers, where I could only hear her gentle voice. My shaman's presence remained with me as I retrieved the rue, notably one of the most protective herbal plants there is. Just holding the rue made my body begin to feel better. I knew this bath was really going to help me. My extremities began to warm and my light-headedness started to dissipate. I had been so assiduous in taking care of my herbs that when I needed them I trusted that they would be there for me. My muscles settled into a more relaxed position and I placed the rue into the bathwater, laying some atop the floating rosemary. I looked into my heart for a prayer and this is what fell from the sky onto my lips:

> *"Almighty Spirit, bring us everlasting life as we embark on our journeys. Heal us from the ills of self and protect our souls from harm. We ask this in accordance with divine righteousness."*

I echoed this prayer a few times. The vibration was so strong that I didn't know if I was going to be able to make a connection with the rue's elemental. I felt an intensity come through the ethers, but no elemental appeared. I thought I must have done something wrong and called out to the shaman to assist me. I waited patiently, and then, through the shaman's vision, I was able to see an energy. This energy was magnificent and had no form. It embellished the rue plant with its essence and stayed ensconced in the ethers so that is powers would remain strong.

There was a light glowing from the bathwater. I now could see my shaman, blessing it, and also enhancing the powers of the elementals and the plants. That was his job. I stepped into the bath and allowed myself to partake in its healing energies for almost an hour. Over the following few days, I recuperated and my symptoms subsided gracefully. I knew I could soon head back to the house.

I started to frequent the home a few times each week, continuing to pray for the lost children. John showed up sometimes to support me. I eventually became stronger when I was there, and my body and spirit would be less affected each time I went. I would bring new cookies and new flowers on occasion, waiting until I knew the energy of the old cookies was eaten and the flowers withered. The energy of the home seemed to brighten with each visit, and my shaman watched over me whenever I went there. As time progressed, I was greeted by laughing children when I walked through the front door. The dead silence and heaviness began to change at the sound of this laughter. I was able to breathe better when I was there, and many of the child spirits were trusting me more. The portal in the living room seemed brighter each time, and souls would walk through it like it was any other opening. As the children healed, I knew that my time there was coming to an end. But it was not yet complete.

The higher the truth, the simpler it is.
—Abraham Isaac Kook

I prayed, asking the shaman to help bring closure. This would be closure for these children, as well as mark a significant physical healing for myself. The miasm was continually being released and raised to the light, and my ancestors were also being freed. The energies that had not allowed me to heal in entirety before were now weakened, and the spirits that we (my spirit guides and I) had been helping thus far were playing an integral part in that.

I prepared myself to go into the house one last time. I sat on my living room floor with my rosebud beaded rosary and meditated. I asked the shaman and the plant world, along with all the saints I pray to, to give me guidance.

As I was praying, I felt a tapping on my shoulder. I turned to see the spirit of an elderly lady. She told me she was a storyteller, a wise woman, who loved to create pottery. She surrounded herself with children, or rather, they followed her wherever she went. She told them stories, and they listened with fervor and never left her side. She showed me that she was the guardian (plant spirit) of the sage plant, and that she would come with me to the house and walk the remainder of the children into the light—those who wanted to go and were ready to go. She asked me to prepare some sage for our journey. I did so immediately.

I drove over to the house, with my tools and what felt like a carload of spiritual helpers. The children always knew when I was coming. I loved coming to that house now. It was joyful.

My shaman was already there, and I could see John out of the corner of my eye, a smile on his face. I'd brought some more cookies, and set them down on the floor. This felt like a celebration. The elderly woman, the storyteller, was at my side. I sat and went into a meditative space as the woman began to tell stories. The children gathered near her one by one, curious, to listen. They held on to her gray woolen skirt, whose train seemed to travel miles on the etheric floor.

In the background was my shaman. He silently lowered his head and breathed his prayer. He indicated that I should gather my sage and bring it forward to the middle of the room. With one breath, he breathed a prayer to imbue the sage and the elderly woman with the intensity of powers they had never known before. He was benevolent, merciful toward the child spirits.

> *"Grandmother, we open our arms to take in your*
> *wisdom. Let us not be foolish in our ways. Heal us*
> *from impatience and ignorance. Help us to walk the*
> *path of righteousness with Spirit. Guide us, and help*
> *us to guide those who come after us. We pray to you,*
> *O Grandmother, that we may be made humble and*
> *pass on your wisdom."*

I watched. The shaman sang those words with ardor. And the elderly woman distilled her storytelling magic. The auras around the children became lighter, and my body was starting to beam. The energetic cords that had been attaching the children and myself were falling apart, and my physical and energetic bodies were lighter. We were in the midst of splendor, and the home had never felt so enchanting.

Having received her blessings from the shaman and the Creator, the elderly woman gently picked up the train of her woolen skirt from the floor. The children held on with all their being. She walked through the living room, glancing at the children with a smile. Never once halting the magical words of her story, she took them gracefully through the portal. The aroma of the sage plant filled the air, and even the cookies seemed to be acknowledged as their life force was taken. The house began to quiet as the last of the child spirits walked through that portal. I turned to see where my shaman was. He had already departed.

I sat in the room for a moment, by myself, still on the floor. I just looked around. The room was neither empty nor full—it just was there. I didn't hear any laughter or crying. I actually didn't hear anyone talking to me or connecting with me from the other side. It was as though what had just transpired had never taken place.

I picked up my belongings and went home.

I slept well over those next few days. My body was healing, and my spirit was elated. I called the owner of the home to let him know that I no longer needed to come to his house anymore. He told me that, a few days after I was last there, part of the bedroom ceiling had collapsed. I had predicted as much. The energy matrix for the lost children was broken, and I trusted that it was also broken for myself. Now it was time for me to heal those broken cords and undo some of the chaos that had been done. I had not been able to break the pattern before I met the shaman, but for some reason, this was all meant to happen the way in which it did.

During my morning meditations, some of the children would continue to pass by to say hello. But they were no longer stuck. They came by just to let me know they missed me and that they were doing fine.

I felt freer inside and ready to learn more from my shaman about his work with plant spirit healing. He let me know that sometime soon, we would visit the countryside and do more work with souls and plants. That is where I would learn most of what I needed to know about his plant spirit magic. Until that time, however, he wanted me to focus on practicing, with my clients, what I had learned so far, and also on repairing my health at a cellular level—the pesticides were ready to exit my nervous and immune systems. I knew that he was right; through seeing clients, my own healing process would continue.

My Client Work

Becky

Becky called me one day to schedule a session. I had never met her before. When she arrived for her appointment, I saw that she was a beautiful, middle-aged European woman who was struggling with asthma and bronchitis. She worked as a nurse, and was happily married with a few children. She was very devout and prayed often, but the nagging cough and wheezing persisted. I did an intake and learned that she used an inhaler when necessary, but wasn't fond of allopathic medicine and its focus on drugs and surgery. I asked about her family history; she said that her mother was also a pious woman who prayed reverently, and that for some reason she suspected that it was her relationship with her mother that was tying her into her health condition. I communicated with the other side and passed along the information I'd received during the intake, for confirmation.

Becky was relieved by our conversation—someone finally understood her. As we talked, I found that I kept shaking my head and dropping it toward one side, so I asked her who'd had the stroke in her family. Her father had, and he'd survived. Then my lungs became suffused with smoke and I couldn't breathe, so I was curious about which relative was the smoker. Her mother was. As I opened the door to her relatives in the spirit world, it seemed like I was in the middle of a family gathering. I was emphatically picking up various symptoms that my client shared with relatives on the other side. For some reason, her ancestors had decided to make their way into her energy field and finish their earthly work through Becky without her permission. No wonder she was having so many headaches!

When a man does a piece of work which is admired by all we say that it is wonderful, but when we see the changes of day and night, the sun, the moon, the stars in the sky, and the changing seasons upon the earth, with their ripening fruits, anyone must realize that it is the work of someone more powerful than man.
—Chased by Bears,
Santee-Yanktonai Sioux

I needed to figure out Becky's relationship with these ancestors to discover where this pattern had started. After talking some more, I found out that her mother, Maria, who was very involved in family matters, had allowed the family to really bulldoze their way into her life and the lives of those immediately around her. This had made her mother sickly and emotionally weak; she felt powerless against the busybodies in the family and didn't have a voice. No one seemed to pay attention to Maria—they just told her what to do all the time. Her addiction to cigarettes had helped her deal with some of her anxieties.

When Maria got married, she married into the same pattern. Her husband didn't respect her and yelled at her all the time. Maria was not a fighter. She would cry often, and run to church and pray. When she had children, she kept them close. She protected them but needed their protection as well. Emotional boundaries were confusing for Maria and her children; she sought out her children as confidants at times. Becky, who was the oldest girl, was the most confused of all the children. Because of Maria's insecurities, she'd inadvertently used Becky as an emotional and energetic shield. Even at age four, Becky would argue and defend her mother if anyone in the family treated her badly. She could feel, even so young, the energy of someone hurting her mother. More importantly, she was able to experience her mother's pain. Becky grew up like this until, in her early twenties, she left home and likewise married young. Luckily she married an emotionally healthy man, but she took on the health and spiritual issues that her family had placed upon her. One of her children even energetically inherited the lung weakness, which developed into repetitive bronchitis.

I needed to work with Becky on developing the proper boundaries. I also needed to work with her ancestors on the same thing. It was also important that Becky express some unresolved grief and anger from her childhood, and that would take some time.

The first thing I wanted to do was give Becky an ally—a plant ally—that she could call upon. Through prayer, she could activate the cellular memory of the plant's healing energies. I felt the energy of my shaman in the ethers; he was present just for support if I needed it. I told Becky that I would ask my guides for an ally for her, and then she could learn how to be in relationship with it.

I held her hand and prayed, and gold energy filled my psychic vision. Off in the distance, I saw what appeared to be a Catholic saint. How perfect, since Becky and her family were devout Catholics. I looked closer and saw that it was St. John the Baptist—and then I knew that the plant he was holding for Becky was St. John's wort.

I heard my prayer in my heart and began to speak its words:

> *"Divine Truth, shed for us healing waters through your many tears. Shed for us the breath of life through your blood. Deliver us into the grace of eternal life. Grant us peace within."*

The energy of those words surrounded Becky until she felt a calm come over her. She sensed a lightness around her, and I told her it was the energy bestowed by St. John's wort.

I prayed to the shaman, too, and asked him to bless the healing session. What happened next was similar to what I'd experienced when my shaman first conducted a healing on me: not only did elementals from the plant world appear, but anointed ones in the spirit world, who had the capacity to intensify the healing effect of plant spirit medicine, also made their presence known. They seemed to like Becky very much and wanted to help her feel better. The elementals seemed to be whirling around her, while the shaman, along with another medicine man trained in oriental healing arts and a Native American healer, graced the room we were sitting in. All I had done was open up the space for these beings to come and assist. I watched, as all who were present worked on the issues Becky was struggling with.

Becky coughed a little, and, as the work was being done, she began to talk about her childhood and her mother. She loved her mother immensely. She remembered her mom and dad yelling all the time and how, after a while, her mother just gave up fighting. It wasn't worth it to her, and she began to withdraw from conflict and internalize her anger. Becky had watched as her mother was criticized and cast away by various family members. When Becky asked her mom why the family was so mean to her, Maria couldn't give her an answer. From the time Becky was young and her mom seemed

God founded the Earth with wisdom and established the heavens with understanding.
—Proverbs 3:19

to give up, she became Maria's voice and protected her. As Becky got older, her father was hard on her as well, but her mom failed to defend her when Becky felt she needed it. But Becky had a voice and was a fighter.

Tears were rolling down Becky's face as she relayed these memories to me, and her breathing became a little hampered. She started to have a panic attack, so I told her to recall the energy of the beginning of the session, when I'd prayed and she'd felt calm. She did so, and with that, the gold light and some of the beings appeared to reinforce what she needed. Becky could feel this, even though she wasn't able to see what was going on.

She waited a few minutes until her panic subsided, and then continued to recall her painful past. She remembered one experience in particular: once, when she was a teenager, she came home past her curfew and her father went into a rage. Her mother actually tried to defend her, but to no avail—her father was stronger. Becky was angry with her mother for not being as powerful as her father, and said that it was that way for her most of her life. She wept, not just for herself, but for her mom.

After all these years, she was still carrying her mother. This was evident when Maria's spirit appeared behind her. Although Maria was still alive at the time, her spirit was able to join us at that moment. It came through as both her higher self and her lower self. When Becky was recalling the trauma of her childhood, I could see Maria in the background, crying and hiding in the corner of my vision. In spirit, she appeared to be a pale and unnerved woman. Her life force was diminished. That was her lower self—the part of her that was still stuck in the past somehow and could not let its trauma be healed.

When Becky could finally release and have a good cry and affirm her love for her mother, Maria's higher self appeared.

She came in much lighter and brighter at that point. Her face was soft and filled with compassion and concern for her daughter. She energetically filled the room with hugs for Becky in the hopes that Becky could feel them. I was working with Becky's spirit in the hope that she could reconcile with that part of herself that felt loved, safe, and powerful, all the while invoking the St. John's wort healing magic.

It was important for me to work with Maria, too, so that the negativity that caused her soul to be stuck could be undone—and so that eventually, she could let go of Becky. Becky also needed to let go of her mom when the time was right. We talked about that at length, and Becky had much homework to do. Her grief and rage were at times immeasurable, so I suggested that she start a journal while remembering to call upon the healing energies of St. John's wort, which we'd invoked at the start of the session. Writing would help her express what she could not express verbally.

Becky left with an abundance of things to do before we met again. I knew that the energy of St. John's wort would stay with her until she no longer needed it.

When Becky came back a few weeks later, she was lighter. She mentioned that she and her mom went out to dinner one evening and enjoyed themselves; Becky remarked that her mom was a bit different, as if a small amount of weight had been taken off her shoulders. She was keeping a journal, and we looked it over. Becky read me passages that embraced the past, the present, and her hopes for the future. She'd talked mostly about her mom in the early entries, and then started to focus on herself. She told me she would meditate and remember to ask the St. John's wort to be present, and try to allow herself to receive the same energies that she had experienced during our first time together. Becky was on her way to healing.

We met a number of times over the next year. Becky was growing stronger in herself, developing better boundaries with her mother and taking better care of herself. She enrolled in some art classes and focused on simply eating better and exercising. Little by little, she was letting go of her mom, and little by little, her health was improving. She began to become aware of the times when her asthma and bronchitis were triggered, and did her best to try to heal it. She was able to bring herself into a meditative space more easily as the time passed, and grew accustomed to always being surrounded by healing energies. To her surprise, she found herself enjoying the time she spent with her mother, not feeling burdened anymore by her mother's emotions.

Becky was now able to see her mom as separate from herself, and worked effortlessly to have compassion for her from a different place within. After we stopped meeting, I heard that Becky was enjoying her life to the fullest and continuing to take very good care of herself. I also heard that her mother passed, and I knew that both Becky and Maria were now free.

If a man would pass through Paradise in a dream, and have a flower presented to him as a pledge that his soul had really been there, and if he found that flower in his hand when he awoke—Aye! and what then?
—Samuel Taylor Coleridge

Robert

Robert walked into my Connecticut office in the wintertime. The first time we met turned out to be a very interesting session. He supposedly came because his physicians had diagnosed him with early rectal cancer, but he wanted to talk about many other things. The cancer was the last thing on his mind that day.

Mainly, Robert wanted to know all there was to know about God and the angels. I was stupefied. He literally had a list of questions; the first was whether God loved him, and how I knew that. He also wanted to know if God forgave him for all the mistakes he'd made in his life. I knew at that point that Robert was going to be a special client, and indeed he was. It turns out he had a wife and children and loved them dearly. He was also very passionate about his work, and enjoyed his life very much. But despite all that, he was carrying around a deep-seated sense of self-rejection. He smoked marijuana often, in small hits, so that he could try to open up to those states of consciousness that he was now asking me about.

Robert and I spent all of that first session talking about God. Messages came through from the other side regarding his life, his thoughts, his dreams. Robert needed a lot of convincing that God loved him. He asked me if I thought God was angry about his mistakes. I told him that God loved him and wasn't angry in the way that he perceived he was. It was like Robert was trying to prove, to himself and to me, that he was unworthy of any kind of unconditional love from a higher power. He believed that his family and friends loved him, but he could not believe in a God who loved him.

As our conversation progressed, I sensed that Robert had a lot of rage toward his father. He'd mentioned briefly that his dad was very controlling and wanted him to be perfect. Robert had pursued his father's affections and approval for most of his life, but never seemed to get it. He often felt judged, and this affected the way he lived in the world. I could tell that he feared masculine energy and ended up rebuking it within himself. He couldn't assimilate love of self and love from a higher power. Because he viewed God as a masculine energy (as opposed to a feminine one), he accepted the notion that he was unable to receive or be worthy of any kind of love from above. He felt like he existed without form at times.

Robert spent his life testing himself, testing God, and testing all the masculine relationships in his life. Feminine relationships were manageable for him—for the most part he enjoyed his female friendships and adored the women in his family. He was allowing feminine energy to dominate his masculine side, so there was an unhealthy balance.

Robert didn't want to explore his past in too much detail, since he felt there was no need to at the present time. I was brief on the topic, just mentioning offhand how some of his relationship with his dad played a role in how he related to himself. Robert wasn't ready to hear that, not did he have any interest in it. He just wanted to focus on his relationship with God.

I did the best I could during our hour. Robert had a quizzical look on his face whenever I spoke. When our time was done, he thanked me graciously and left the office. I wasn't sure what to make of our meeting, so left it at that.

A year passed, and I didn't hear back from Robert until he called to schedule another appointment, asking if I remembered him. Of course I did; I said I would be happy to work with him again.

When he walked into my office, he seemed angry. He was angry with me, with everyone, with God. He asked why, at our previous meeting, I hadn't seen or told him that his cancer would progress rapidly and that his prognosis would be grim. After all, I was an intuitive medium and I should have known that. I responded by saying that I understood he was angry, and that when he came to see me a year ago, he hadn't wanted to discuss the cancer during the session. Furthermore, even if he'd wanted to, I'm not God and cannot see everything when a person comes to me. No medium or psychic can.

At this point, Robert's cancer had spread further into his intestinal tract and liver. He had undergone a few surgeries and was also going through chemotherapy. He looked desperate, and destitute of spirit. When I looked into his eyes, I saw defiance—defiance toward God and toward his inner knowing; a power struggle. It was all part of the process he was working through. When I asked him why he had come back, he said he wanted to talk more about God. Once again, he wanted to feel God loving him, to know that God loved him. And, significantly, he wanted to look at how his father had made him feel all of his life.

I thought we should begin by talking about his dad in a little more depth. I asked him to help me understand his father in his own words. Michael, Robert's dad, was a retired military man. He and his wife had only one child and settled in a suburb in western New York. Michael was not a hands-on dad, so to speak. It was Robert's mom who reared him for most of his life and gave him the emotional nourishment he needed. Michael was a very silent man for the most part, which was how he controlled Robert. Whenever he spoke with Robert, it was to criticize him for something that had just occurred; he would not say anything at all if Robert was looking for some feedback. Michael was an empty soul, and Robert did whatever he could to gain his approval, as opposed to silence or a few words of disdain.

Whatever befalls the Earth, befalls the sons of Earth. Man does not weave the web of life, he is merely a strand in it. Whatever he does to the web, he does to himself.
—Chief Seattle

Robert thought it was his fault that he was never acknowledged or received by his father. Although his mother saw what was going on and tried to distract him to make him feel better, this only served to increase and validate Robert's growing anger. He spent most of his young and early adult life living this pattern.

His way of dealing with it was the marijuana that he'd started smoking at a pretty young age. He wanted to know if he'd caused his cancer. I told him no, and I was not going to let him use that as an excuse to further punish himself for not being "good enough."

I had my work cut out for me—Robert was convinced that he was unworthy of love and healing. It wasn't time to work with plant medicine yet, since I felt we needed to make him a little stronger first. I went over his diet with him, and suggested some nutrition, supplementation, and strengthening and detoxification techniques that he could do at home. Robert was already seeing a number of holistic practitioners as well as allopathic medical doctors. He wanted to get as much support and information as he could to help him on his journey. He had a therapist, acupuncturist, holistic MD, and various other healing artists. He would even talk about them in session and ask me if I thought they were helping him. I would reply by asking him if *he* thought they were.

Robert scheduled sessions with me every two weeks. We kept to that schedule until the day he died, three years later. We worked slowly, and, through our sessions, continued to explore his family dynamics and relate them to how he saw himself in this world. For the first few months, although he left every session thanking me, he wasn't sure if the sessions were helping at all. Although he didn't know if he believed in anything I said, he returned time after time. Each time, he told me that he'd done what I'd suggested, as well as followed the advice of his numerous other practitioners. But he couldn't tell if any of it was making a difference.

Then there was a session, a few months after we'd started, when Robert walked in with a gleam in his eye. I asked him what was different. He said something had begun to shift within him, and he thought he was beginning to feel the presence of God around him. I asked how he knew. He said he'd started to feel a calm in his heart, and wanted more. He felt a serenity about at him at times when things were chaotic, and he didn't know where it was coming from. He wanted to feel and know this energy in every aspect of his life, and wanted to try to garner more of this higher power. What he didn't realize was that this power had been within him all along. But Robert still wasn't ready for a plant spirit—I wanted to do some work with his father first.

During one session, I had Robert on the table for some hands-on energy and cranial work. I asked him to think about his father and tell me about events from his child-hood that he still held resentment about. He didn't need to tell me aloud; I just wanted to observe his energy body and see what reaction his father's spirit would have. As Robert started to visualize these childhood stories in his head, his energy field shifted and his organs pulsed rapidly. His eye-lids were flickering back and forth and he twitched on the massage table. I looked over my shoulder as I felt his father's spirit draw near. I asked, telepathically, what his father wanted from him and why he wouldn't let Robert go.

Michael proceeded to tell me that he loved his son but had been very disappointed in him ever since he could remember; that it felt like no matter what Robert did, Michael was aware that he could not connect with his son on the level he wanted to. I asked Michael about his rela-tionship with his own father, and he showed me pictures of a similar relationship, one in which his own father disowned him. This was something that Michael had never gotten over, and since he never rooted himself in a healthy paternal relationship with his own dad, he did not have the tools or the desire to do so with his own son. He grieved because he realized he had nothing to offer Robert. When I asked him again why he was holding on to his son, he said it was the only way he was able to deal with his feelings about his own father. Michael knew that Robert carried a lot of anger toward him—Robert had vented it from time to time. And while Robert had at least had some opportunity to express his anger at his father, Michael, having been disowned, had not. Through Robert, Michael was able to have some sort of connection with his own dad, a sort of emotional incest if you will. I talked with Michael while my hands were still working on the back of Robert's head; Robert fell into a gentle sleep.

I asked Michael if he wanted to learn how to relate to his own feelings, and if he wanted his son to be free of some pain. He said yes. I told him that while my focus was on his son, I would give him some tools to help him on his journey.

I called in my shaman and asked him to help. I asked him to guide me to the best plant medicine to help with this family dynamic. The room became still, with Robert still in a sleep/dreamtime space. My breathing became labored for a few moments, then cleared, and an energy seemed to whirl up the front of my body and into my head, making me dizzy. I heard myself mumbling some syllables—magical syllables. I knew a plant prayer and invocation were coming.

"Rod of light, cast down upon us your invincible power of God. Through the Holy Spirit, manifest the truth of all things hidden and unseen."

My voice grew deeper and louder and I repeated the prayer.

"Rod of light, cast down upon us your invincible power of God. Through the Holy Spirit, manifest the truth of all things hidden and unseen."

I've never inhaled and exhaled so deeply in my life. With my shaman present, Robert still in twilight, and Michael's spirit hovering, another spirit approached our space.

It was a male soul who had lived on earth hundreds of years ago and was somehow connected to the plant kingdom. When he died, he apparently left a number of issues in his life uncompleted. He'd walked the earth's gardens in spirit for centuries, and one of the plants he'd befriended, along with its elementals, was the skullcap. The elementals loved this soul and literally took him under their wings. He'd received much comfort from them and seemed to make nature, especially the skullcap plant, his new home. It was his own heaven. He took care of the gardens he came across and made a vow to assist others in bringing completion to their life stories. Between the earth's spiritual gardens and the clouds, he kept himself pretty busy—heaven's gardener, of sorts.

This spiritual gardener appeared to be very joyful and light of soul, and he took Michael by his energy field and danced around. He showed Michael his gardens, and then led him down memory lane, showing him scenes of the arguments Michael had had with Robert, and how they'd both felt afterward. Michael was saddened by the memories, but the gardener pressed on. He wanted Michael to begin to acknowledge some of his own pain. As always, what felt like hours took only minutes in real time. Then he led Michael back to his garden and brought him near the skullcap. He transmitted the energy of the skullcap onto Michael's spirit, which began to cry. The skullcap was able to penetrate some of the emotional wall that had built up.

Michael looked at his son Robert, still sleeping on my table, and compassion filled his eyes. The gardener and Michael then exchanged some words that I couldn't hear, and the gardener left. I saw the gleam still in Michael's eye and asked him if he was ready to let his son go. He said yes.

I wished him well as he disappeared into the ethers.

When you care for one tree, all the trees smile.

—Laura Silvana Aversano

Robert seemed to be waking. He didn't realize that he'd fallen asleep. He said he'd dreamt something about his father, but couldn't remember what. He got up from the table and said he felt that presence again, that calm in his heart. When he thought about his father, he didn't feel as enraged as before.

Weeks turned into months and months turned into years. Robert and I continued to do work about his father, and I would psychically call in the skullcap plant to assist Robert when he was stuck. I didn't tell him about the healing energies of this plant, but used it whenever he took a step back. If it was good for his father, and the relationship with his dad was the source of the original wounding, then I knew the skullcap would also benefit Robert and protect him when his father's lower self would come in—if it did at all.

Robert was healing, and I was elated. He seemed freer than he ever had in his life, and was learning to detach himself in a healthy way from the traumatic memories of his past. He also learned, over the years we worked together, to have compassion for himself and forgive himself for what he thought he'd contributed to the abusive relationship. His stride came back and he felt confident that his cancer would be healed. I knew only that his spirit was healing, as was the pattern that had helped create his malady—but I reserved judgment on the progression of his cancer, as I always felt that it was between him and God.

Our sessions were varied and we began to focus more on Robert's life as a whole, not just his childhood. One day, Robert came to me and he said he wanted to stop the chemotherapy and the cancer-fighting drugs he was on. He had been through so many treatments and had had chemotherapy on and off for years. Now that he felt emotionally so much freer, he wanted to be free of the disciplined regime of cancer fighting as well. He asked me what I thought, and I told him that I couldn't make that decision for him. He understood, and said that he needed to go with his gut. So he stopped all forms of allopathic treatment and decided to continue with only a handful of holistic practitioners, I being one of them. He even took a break from our sessions for a month or so, and then came back. He just needed some time to have fun, as much as his body would let him.

Robert deteriorated quickly after stopping his previous regime. I had a feeling he knew that he would. I got a call from him saying that he didn't think he had long now. He was immobilized in a hospital bed in a hospice, with the tender care of nurses and his family by his side. I went to see him. His skin seemed shrunk down to his bare bones, and flesh hung from every wasting muscle. But I didn't focus on that—I only focused on the bright light around him. I asked how he was doing and he said he was okay. To my surprise, he asked again if God loved him. I told him, unequivocally, yes. I saw the spirits of his ancestors in the room, and let him know that they would be there when he was ready to cross, and that even though he was afraid, he would not be alone. I promised him that it would not be as frightening as he expected, and that as he got closer, he would begin to see all the spirits I saw and simply leave his body and walk with them. I asked him if there was anything else he needed from me, and he said he wanted me to make sure his family was okay afterwards. I told him I would do that.

I knew that now, at last, was the time to offer Robert plant magic to help his transition. We had worked together for so long that he'd gotten used to my quirkiness. I meditated for a moment, and gently said the prayer that came to me.

"We call on you, ancestors of the earth and sky. Hear our prayers. We thirst for wholeness. We hunger for nourishment. And when we are ready to come home to the Great Spirit in the sky, carry us on your wings and fly."

Robert laughed, as he always did if he thought my work was too esoteric. But being the amazing sport that he always was, he went with it. His curiosity still intact, he inquired as to which spirit I was calling in now. He knew I worked with plant medicine, so he was not totally in shock when I said that I was calling on a plant for him and wanted him to call upon it himself during his transition, whenever he felt afraid. He was okay with the proposition. I laughed with him and echoed my prayer again. Then I saw, upon the bare white walls of his hospice room, a medicine man. He was chanting and holding a piece of mugwort in his hand. He was perched on a rock over a blazing fire. I stared at the fire for a bit and, interestingly enough, Robert said he started to feel some warmth come over his body—he thought it had something to do with what I was working with. I hadn't told him of the vision yet. I watched as the medicine man drew the plant to his mouth and forehead, each time reiterating prayers for the earth and for those who were dying. His special gift involved assisting souls in crossing over. I wanted to respect his space, and was not intrusive. I pulled my energy back from the vision and humbly asked that this spirit be there for Robert when he needed him. I did not get an answer, but I knew that I was heard, and I had faith that my request would be honored.

I turned to Robert and told him what I'd experienced. He laughed again. I knew I would be hearing that laugh for the last time. I instructed him to call upon the mugwort plant, and also the vision as he remembered it through my experience. I said that every time he did, he would feel as peaceful as he did now. We actually laughed some more. I gave him a hug goodbye and told him I would check in with him to see how he was doing when he got to the other side.

As I walked out of the room, I wanted to burst into tears. But I remained composed, since I needed to spend a few minutes with his family.

Robert crossed over a few days later. He was still laughing. I could hear it echoing through the heavens.

The Appalachians

In addition to utilizing my new plant healing knowledge to help clients, I continued to practice my work in other ways as well. It proved to be an invigorating privilege bestowed upon me by the spirit world. My body had gained much of its strength back and the miasm was almost completely healed.

Summertime was upon us, and I wanted to plant some of the plants that kept popping into my mind. I had a very small plot of land behind my home, not enough for a big garden, but enough for me to plant the thirty or so plants I kept thinking about.

I took a trip to an herbal gardening store in Connecticut and picked up some of what I needed. I ordered some of the more exotic annuals online. I cleared my soil and nourished it. I didn't leave much room in between my plantings; in my excitement, I had overestimated how much space I really had. After planting the seedlings, I smudged my garden. I sat there every day for two weeks and smudged, prayed, and even sang songs, using my rattle for accompaniment (living as I did in a tight-knit suburb of New York City, I knew my neighbors would think I was nuts, but I didn't care). My sister came to visit when I was putting the seedlings in the ground, and when she visited again two weeks later, the seedlings had literally grown over a foot. She was astonished, and asked them what kind of miracle plant food I had given them. I told her that I'd smudged with sage, prayed, and rattled. She just laughed and said no more.

I knew that these plants were going to be the basis for a book I would write, and that later on, I would be spiritually journeying with the plants I had grown, asking for the healing remedies they could offer. It was one thing to always have been given remedies by the spirit world; it was another to be invited in—by the plant kingdom and the plant gods—as a conduit for another type of healing work. I was excited, even more so than before. I would be able to put their healing magic into words and share them with others.

I continued to nourish my plants until it was time for the next piece of my work to begin. The first leg of this spiritual journey took me to the foothills of the Appalachian Mountains. My shaman had told me that some of the work we would be doing would involve actual traveling, and that some of the remedies would be dispensed in mountainous countryside. And thus it came to be.

Circumstances led me, that summer, to over two hundred acres of unspoiled acreage. I was to spend a week there immersed in nature. The pine trees endlessly traversed the hills, and the presence of ancient spirits was obvious. Many could still hear their footsteps, and their imprints were the breath of the land. The oaks stood tall and majestic, unwavering at my delight upon arrival. I could actually feel their excitement as golden rays of sunlight poured down onto their branches. Out of the corner of my eye, I spotted a great horned own hovering above, as though it knew I was coming and was watching my every move.

During the day, the air was warm and sultry. The nights were cool and awe-inspiring. I slept well the first night I arrived, awaking at the crack of dawn to begin my work. I took a journal with me, my rattle, some sage and other protective herbs, and gifts for the spirit world. I hadn't a clue where to begin, so I kept vigil as those in the spirit world guided me to the ground that I would pray upon.

I sat in the middle of a lustrous, overgrown hillside, the grass almost as tall as I was. There was no other human being around. But every living creature knew I was there, and every spirit knew as well. I took my tools from my satchel and began to pray. I went into a deep meditative space and my psychic vision became very refined. I told the spirits of the land why I was there—that I was meant to learn more about plant medicine and be of service if they needed me. I had to gain their trust, and realized it wasn't going to be easy.

I looked around as I prayed, and began to get glimpses of times past. I saw animals, mostly deer, that had starved to death on that land. They were running around in spirit, their bodies emaciated and malnourished, searching desperately for food. This took me aback a little, as I was not used to seeing animal spirits this way. Then the visions started to become clearer. Bloodshed—war between the Native Americans and the white men—and women and children lost and frightened. I could not forget the sight of the women and children (throughout my time in the mountains, they were perhaps the friendliest). I didn't see the medicine men or warriors at first; the male spirits of the land seemed to stay clear of me at the beginning, until I could prove my worthiness.

We don't see things as they are. We see things as we are.
—Anaïs Nin

I stayed on the hillside throughout the afternoon, taking notes on what I was observing. Some of the Native children had been left motherless, and some of the mothers were left without their children. This reminded me of some of the lost children I had worked with. My shaman was somewhere in the ethers, but this was not his territory. He respected the domain of other souls and had pulled his energy back from me.

The friends I was staying with told me of a plot of land where they had tried in earnest to cultivate vegetation, but to no avail. That first afternoon, I walked over to that ground and saw that is was sacred. There had been mass killings of women and children on that parcel, and their souls continued to wander.

I wasn't too happy about what I had seen that first day, and could only wonder what the rest of my trip would bring. I decided one of the first things to do was to ask my friends if they had any extra food for the deer spirits that had starved on that land. They did, and the next afternoon we took a walk, throwing the food down and letting the deer spirits know it was solely for them. I let my friends continue to do that while I tried to make contact with some of the women and children I'd seen. I sat and thought about the best way to approach this, remembering my lost children who had crossed over. I called upon them, any of them, to come and assist me. In just moments, pieces of my hair were being pulled and, oh, their laughter was so contagious and memorable. I asked them to befriend the children that I was seeing here, to play with them. While they did that, I focused on befriending the women.

Surrounded by all the native flora, I put on my gloves and carefully harvested a handful of nettles growing near me. I held it up to my heart and started to hum. The hum-

ming came so easily, as sparrows circled above and butterflies fluttered about with their dew-drenched wings.

> *"O loving kindness, drench the fires of our bit-*
> *terness and scorn. Weep not, for the ills of the human*
> *heart can only be appeased by your unbounded gra-*
> *cious love."*

My heart expanded with love for the nettles and, obviously,
for the women and children I was seeing. I waited with
anticipation for the plant elemental or deva to appear, and
lo and behold, tickling my ear were two delightful fairies. I
wasn't expecting fairies in the midst of all this wounding, but
there they were, bright and bold. They were radiating love,
gentleness, tenderness, all of the feelings that were channel-
ing through me. These fairies were supporting one another,
exchanging healing energies one at a time and glowing in
response to the gifts being offered. I just went with it, in the
hopes that the souls of these women and children would see
the fairies and come closer to me. I truly needed to leave this
in God's hands.

I played with the fairies. They frolicked around me,
and my lost children knew to come near. They had already
befriended some of the Native children and motioned them
to come over to where the fairies were playing. As in earth
reality, if a child wanders, a mother will follow. Even though
some of the Native children in the spirit world were motherless, the other mothers took care of them. When the mothers and children had died, trauma had caused some of their
souls to become stuck in some unidentifiable dimension
of the spirit world, while the others had indeed manage to
cross into the light, and, with tireless effort, were trying to
reunite with their loved ones.

The lost children dallied a bit, until they knew that the
Native children's souls were behind them, and then one and

all danced around the pine tree. I said hello to the Native children and then just sat where I was, so as not to frighten them. The mothers came over and looked at me from a few yards away. I smiled gently and wanted them to know I was no threat to them. Spirits are always curious when someone on this side of the veil can see them.

I kept the tone of my voice gentle while I told them that I would do what I could to help them. I said I didn't know how yet, but I had been led there to do some work and, prayerfully, the guides who helped me thus far would support my endeavors on behalf of the souls wandering that land. I wondered, though, if I had overstepped my bounds, because I knew there were literally thousands of souls on that land. I only saw hundreds by the time I left, but I felt certain that thousands were lost. I was befuddled. I had been in that place before, not knowing why I was where I was I was or what I was supposed to do about it. But I watched as the women and children took care of one another, and they watched me. I left them in peace, telling them I would be back the next day to talk with them.

I felt a little relieved that evening before going to bed. I'm not sure why, exactly. I guess I felt I was making some headway, even though I still had no precise direction.

The tree which moves some to tears of joy is, in the eyes of others, only a green thing that stands in the way. . . . As a man is, so he sees.
—William Blake

I was ravenous the next morning and cooked a hearty breakfast. I went out into the fields early to find my new acquaintances. The women and children were out, and they were playing. My lost children were still there as well, and even more fairies were fluttering around. I looked at the deer spirits. They didn't look as emaciated as they did when I'd first arrived, and their coloring was a little better (as best as one can perceive coloring on the other side of the veil). That made my heart warm. I sat with my journal and my rattle and thought I would start out by working with some of the plants growing around me. I'd assumed that the main reason I was there was to gather medicinal and spiritual information about some of the plants I would use for my book, while also knowing that if I was going to help any spirits, this would be the way to do it.

I wanted to embrace every living thing, and every soul near me. I wanted to feel the strength of the pine tree roots reaching far into the unadulterated earth. I wanted to soar like the red-tailed hawks that encircled the sky above me. I wanted to shine in the brilliant sun like the dainty flowers of the chamomile plant. I wanted to be a part of everything around me. In seeing how hungry the deer were, how frightened the Native children seemed, the desperation those mothers of long ago still carried in their souls, I needed to somehow reconcile the beauty I was beholding before me with the wounds of the past I was also seeing. I begged the medicine spirits of the land to help me, to show me a way to embrace the world that they had known, and to let me offer, through my prayers, any solace that might be obtained.

I always knew that the only power there is comes from God. The privilege that we all receive is the privilege to pray, and to do so abundantly. The gift I was given before birth was to be a window and conduit for the other side, but that gift would be of no use if the efficacy of prayer wasn't tapped into. So I prayed, dearly and profusely.

As I was praying, a male soul, slight of frame, with thin, chiseled features and long gray hair, came walking out of the woods. I had no idea who he was. He didn't say a word. He just came up to me and signaled for me to follow him. I was led to a cave, where I sat outside and waited as he disappeared. I had a sense he would come back shortly. I looked at my surroundings and all was still. Then the male spirit reappeared with a number of other male spirits. I didn't recall feeling that uncomfortable before, even in ordinary reality. They circled around me, looked at me, and were reticent in their opinions about me. I waited, and slowly, I began to receive information about what happened to some of the Natives and why the souls were having trouble crossing over. I received this information the same way I usually do, through words, pictures, and kinesthetic feelings. Some of the same pictures flashed through my mind: the strife, the famine, the deprivation, the abuse of the women and children, the loss of the land. The medicine healers and spirits of old were continuing their work on the other side, on behalf of those souls who were stuck, and there were more, many more of their people to help. In many religious and spiritual traditions, a living human being whose prayers can reach the heavens is also needed to help with the transition of these stuck souls. There is a Biblical reference about when two or more are gathered in His name... which can include souls here and in the spirit world.

I was shown some of the tools the medicine men used to use, and some of the games that they would all play as a tribe. I was also given permission by some of the male spirits to work on their land, while the others looked on reluctantly. I thanked them for their trust in me, and left.

I went back to where the children and their mothers were playing and sat in the tall grass once again. I drew my rattle up toward the sky and rejoiced, shaking it gently to the beat of the earth I was sitting on.

I looked at a pine tree and wanted to know its medicine. I tuned in to it, moving my hands and feet to become its limbs. I made myself focus strongly on the scent of its needles, so that the aroma could penetrate my being. I hummed whatever melody came out of my mouth and, grabbing my notebook, started to scribble what the pine tree and the spirits of the pine tree were telling me.

*... Pine medicine... helps you find your way
when you've lost your sense of direction. Needles were
burned to give elders visions. Heals infections of the
lungs, throat, ears. Aids in uterine hemorrhaging.
Brings the spirit back into the body...*

One by one, I would touch a tree, tune in to an animal, grab
hold of a plant or a flower, touch the earth; whatever I did,
I would receive information on the medicinal and spiritual
healing qualities of the living things around me.

*... Prickly ash... used in cases of fevers, chills,
epidemics. Healed heart troubles, headaches, confusion, hysteria. Brought healing to strife among married partners and relationship issues...*

*... White Oak... sacred tree, divination tree, has
powers of prophecy, protection, clearing of evil spirits,
respiratory ailments, male reproductive ailments...*

Deer, elk, wolf medicine—hours passed as I recorded what
I heard, felt, or saw. Whether it was the spirit of a particular
thing, or the spirits that protected it, didn't matter.

I was exhausted by nightfall, and when I looked up to see
the children and the mothers still playing, it looked as though
they were exhausted, too. Something was happening to their
spirits, but I hadn't a clue at that time as to what. I gathered
myself and wearily walked back to the house. I turned to look
behind me as I neared my friends' home because I thought I
heard music playing—flute music. I knew there wasn't a soul
around for miles; my friends had acquired over a hundred
acres of that sacred land, and theirs was the only home on it.
I decided I must be hearing things, or that my friends were
playing the music.

As I climbed the last hill to the house, the music continued. How lovely, I thought. My friends must have put on

a CD and blasted the music at an incredible volume. But when I walked into the house, there was a deadening silence. So much so that I called out to ask if anyone was there. My friend came out of her bedroom and asked me what was wrong. When I asked whether they had been playing any type of flute or Native American music, she looked at me, bewildered, and said no—why? I told her what I'd heard, and she said that it was impossible—there wasn't another home around for miles.

Impossible, or a gift from the spirit world?

I took a long hot shower and went over my notes. I knew my time in the mountains was short, so I wanted to wake up early and get the day started.

At breakfast the next day, my friends asked how my work was going. They also wanted to know if there was anything I could do to improve that parcel of land that was resistant to vegetation growth. I told them I would carry their intentions in my prayers that day.

I went down to my usual spot, which was a ten or fifteen minute walk from the house. The spirits started to appear, but a number of the lost children had gone away, as well as a number of the Native children. Hmm … perhaps the lost children had helped them cross over. I also saw that some of the women, some of the mothers, had smiles on their faces. Their banter seemed lighter. I was ecstatic. I looked around for the hungry deer; there hardly were any now, as my friends had been leaving food out and the animal spirits had fed upon the food's energies.

I really and truly felt grateful. I was understanding that, in some way, I was giving a voice to the ancients of this land. I was the voice for the trees, the animals, the children, the women. And in giving them a voice as I journaled their stories, I had somehow helped release them, or at the very least initiated that process. That is why the plant remedies in the second half of this book do not just come from one spirit; they come from all the spirits who were involved in the healing work. I might write of only one spirit, elemental, or plant god appearing at any specific time, but it is thanks to all the souls I encountered, from the beginning of this work, that my plant remedies came to be. I continue to know that I am just a vehicle for Spirit.

I sat down on the sun-drenched grass that morning and took out my notebook. At first I stayed on the outskirts of where the women and children spirits were playing, but it didn't take me long to get up and move closer. I was smiling; I could feel their laughter. The grass was long and the children spirits were moving to and fro. The beauty of their auras was something to behold. I moved my body in rhythm to their beat, as though I wanted to join in on their leisurely game. I was in unison. It was lovely.

I played for a while and then sat down again to begin my work. I brought myself into my usual meditative space and asked the spirits of nature and the plant gods to help me gather whatever information I could. In my mind and heart, I was seeing my book come together. The information I was gathering here, the plants I had planted at home … all of this would culminate in some sort of story and reference guide.

I wanted to understand a bit more about the animal spirits I was seeing. The spirit deer seemed much more at peace. Birds of prey hovered over me in the skies, monitoring my every move. Both in real-world time and in the spirit world, the animals and their spiritual counterparts were joined in harmony, living together naturally. I asked how animal spirit medicine might work in real time. I

> *The old Indian teaching was that it is wrong to tear loose from its place on the earth anything that may be growing there. It may be cut off, but it should not be uprooted. The trees and the grass have spirits. Whatever one of such growths may be destroyed by some good Indian, his act is done in sadness and with a prayer for forgiveness because of his necessities.*
> —Wooden Leg, Cheyenne

knew that various cultures have different perspectives, and I wasn't sure if I was even going to receive an answer from those around me.

I took my journal, pen in hand, and waited for the syllables to come into my ears.

> *... Animal spirits give their powers to persons who use their medicine to benefit themselves and their tribal relations. Each of the four-leggeds has a spirit that walks both the earth and the spirit realm. Each spirit has powers given to it by Great Spirit, and by the ancestors who embodied it in times past ...*

The words continued, letting me know that, in their tradition, when someone needed assistance or protection from an animal spirit, he or she could connect to and embody the animal in physical form, energetically and psychically. To gain a deeper understanding of the animal kingdom, the person would attempt to identify with the animal in its entirety, harnessing its powers in order to actually become one with it. Such identification and connection were useful for traveling the world beyond the earth, below the Spirit, and in any dimension in between. Sometimes the person would take the shape of an animal to retrieve a spirit that was lost or stolen by another. This exchange of form showed all that the two-leggeds were no different than the four-leggeds. All the creatures made by the Great Spirit are one. The more someone practiced this medicine, the more the spirit of the animal and the spirit of the person would become one.

Many times, the animal and its spirit would choose who would carry its energy, and, through initiation, strengthen the carrier with more powers. When a warrior could skillfully move from animal to human form, he was unable to be touched or harmed by another. The strength of one man became like that of a thousand.

Animal spirit medicine was also used to help with everyday ritual and ceremony, personal growth, and initiation. Animal spirits acted as guides, protectors, and divination tools, and were called upon when needed. Animals respect the earth and show humans how to embrace it as healers and caretakers. They guide humans in walking gracefully on the earth in the shadows of the powers that be. If you pay close attention to the wisdom that an animal brings you, you can see far into the future and back into the past regarding how your specific relationship with the earth can benefit the present moment—thus influencing both times to come and times past. Do not take an animal or its medicine for granted, for the moment you cease to acknowledge the animal's powers, you disconnect yourself from the source of your energy. Remember, as above, so below. Animal spiritual energies contribute to our earthly existence. Animals, before humans, knew and appreciated the bounty of Mother Earth and revered her energies. It is only because of them and the Creator that we continue to grow and even have a life-form with which to nourish ourselves. Think about it.

Fusing with an animal's energy was one of the ways in which a person could understand the created world and its Creator, and also the relationships between the animal kingdom and other kingdoms. Once people felt they could conquer the animal kingdom, however, they often felt they could conquer all others, which led them to abandon the respect we owe to the four-leggeds and to the Creator. As human beings, we have to be very watchful of our need for power, and respect the laws of nature as granted from above. Identifying with an animal can also help us understand our role and relationship to power, as given to us by the Creator. There was once a time when humans and animals shared their powers collectively in nature, and when reverence for the Creator was shared evenly.

Present day animals have become wary because humans fail to recognize them as an important and necessary part of their own creation. Men and women derive their instinctual practices and behaviors from animals, and sexual instincts originally derive from the energies of the animal kingdom. Then they evolve, rising up toward the Creator through the plant kingdom, seeking the higher energies of the Divine. Humans often confuse their relationship to themselves as sexual beings with their primal instincts, and cease to acknowledge a higher sexual aspiration toward the heavens. The primal instincts of the animal kingdom, however, are in fact meant to lead to the awareness of the magic of creation—through the energies that the plant kingdom offers. It is the shared process of awakening, of moving from birth to death, that connects the animal kingdom to the plant kingdom. It is how the story of creation gives rise to the powers and manifestations of the Creator. It is how all things connect and open to the heavens.

We know ourselves to be made of this earth. We know this earth is made from our bodies. For we see ourselves. And we are nature. We are nature seeing nature.
—Susan Griffin

The animal spirit is meant to bridge the world so that humans can enter into alternate realities. It differs from the plant spirit in its intention and essence. Whether or not a traveler knows this, every human is protected by some form of spiritual energy that embraces nature. But sometimes people refuse to utilize all their resources when aspiring to the heavens through the natural world.

Animal spirit medicine can also give you knowledge of the plant kingdom. The four-leggeds of the earth were the first to utilize plant spirit medicine, and gave it freely to humans with the understanding that their use of the natural world would be in right relationship to the heavens. When this did not occur, human relationships with both the animal and the plant kingdoms suffered. People now need to once again earn the trust of the natural world.

You cannot honor one kingdom without honoring all.

As the words stopped coming, a butterfly fluttered at the ends of my long hair as they whispered in the gentle breeze. I acknowledged the spirits and gave thanks for the voices and their words. I felt like I had connected more deeply with the spirits of the deer; it seemed there had been a purpose for their suffering.

I got up to stretch my legs and take a brief stroll. I wanted to walk to the barren vegetable garden my friends were concerned about. But there was nothing remarkable about it when I arrived there; it simply looked like dirt in an unplowed field, parched from drought even though every thing else around it was lush. It was about one-fifth of an acre of land. The sun was still shining in splendor on every blade of grass, every tree branch, and every flower around me. Even this desolate piece of land glowed, with the sun's warming rays upon it.

I decided to sit in the middle of the parcel and do some of my work there. My intentions were that I would eventually find out what had happened there. As I lay down my satchel and tools, I became very hot and my body started to itch. I just let it pass through me and focused on the next flower or tree—whatever it was that spirit wanted me to work with. And so I began, one by one, to work with whomever wanted to lend their voice to me.

> *... Red chestnut medicine... used to assist women going through the change of life. Drinking the tea made out of bark used for hysteria. It would call the spirit of the mind back home. Used for miscarriages and for protecting the mother from malevolent spirits when she was grieving for her child...*

... Beech medicine ... used as a blood purifier, for rheumatism and for tuberculosis. Helps with protection in childhood against physical deformity. Paste of the bark used for broken limbs. Paste also healed wounds. Treated childhood vascular ailments ...

... Mulberry Bush ... used to dispel poisons; acts as an emetic. When planted outside of a home, keeps away all unwanted critters. A paste of the berries helps with poison ivy and other skin rashes ...

I took a break for a moment, looking up from my writing to get a breath of fresh air. My hands were so hot from writing, and I'd temporarily stopped noticing the physical sensations I'd experienced when I first sat down. To my surprise, I saw my shaman, standing there and watching with pride as I did my work. I also saw the male spirit I'd met the other day, the one who took me to that cave, as well as a few of the other male spirits who had been there. The women and children spirits were also not far from me, and elementals and devas and other spirits of nature abounded. We all seemed to be in one harmonious interplay. I felt peaceful when seeing those around me so peaceful. It left an ineffable feeling in my heart.

After a long moment, I turned back to my writing. The rush of heat that went through my body again spurred my hand to start taking down notes, and syllables to begin echoing in my ears. The words came and I became one with them.

... Medicine of plant spirits ... in working with the aforementioned, it is not about the curative practice of the plant medicine itself or even its connection with the elemental. Without our commitment to bringing balance to the consciousness of humans in

regards to caretaking of the earth, the medicine means
nothing to the spirit or the plant god who offers it to
you. It is they who need us to take responsibility for
the healing of the earth's peoples, its creatures, and its
land throughout all time. We are the gatekeepers and
if the earth continues to die, then we are responsible
for the death of its spirit and all those spirits who
reside within its many spiritual dimensions...

What I'd just written sent chills down my spine. It is true that when I first began doing this work and would take a leaf from a flowering plant or a piece of branch from a tree to retrieve its medicine, I noticed that after I was finished hearing its voice, the spiritual energy of the living thing in my hand was totally gone. But please know that whenever I took a part of a tree or flower, I asked permission first. Many times, of course, I just tuned in to the flower or tree in order to be its voice.

I felt that I wanted to know more about children—children of the past, the present, and the future. Since they had been around me for a while in my own spiritual process, I was hoping to have some understanding in their role, as understood by the energies around me. The words came:

... Children are a sign of both the past and
things to come. Anyone who has placed black magic
on a child will fall prey to his own making. It was
said that when children were born ill, they had
taken it upon themselves in agreement with the
Great Spirit to carry the ills of the earth, its caretak-
ers, and the ancestors before them. Some of those spe-
cially gifted children will be the great peacemakers
of times to come. Karma carries itself heavily on the
little ones, and what would be their greatest weak-
ness will be their greatest strength as they get older, if

*they chose to utilize the gifts that were given to them
in the midst of their suffering.*

*It is very easy for children to lose sight of their
spirits and give them over to another, as there will
be many who prey on the spirits of young ones.
There is sometimes fear and confusion left over from
the ancestral energies of another soul, which then
embodies itself in the young one. It is up to the elders
of any time continuum to retrieve the spirit of the
young child back from wherever it has departed and
to send away the ancestral energy. It is the responsibility of every elder to watch over a child, whether
or not it belongs to him ...*

I laughed for a moment in recognition. There's a bumper
sticker I always love to see on the back of cars: "It takes a
village to raise a child." The voice I was hearing through the
ethers was saying the same.

I looked up, and oddly enough, it seemed as though
some of the women and children souls had disappeared. I
wasn't worried, because all the other protective souls were still
around me. I assumed the women and children had crossed
while I was writing. No, I was sure of it.

I wrote for a little while longer, and was growing tired.
I ate some of my bag lunch and hoped that with renewed
strength and vigor, I would be able to figure out the cause of
the land's bareness and glean whether any vegetation could
grow on it in the future.

I lay down for a while and let the sun's moist heat brown
my arms and my face. Ever since childhood, I've loved the
feeling of lying on the earth. That, and snowflakes falling,
are my two fondest nature memories. I always felt so secure,
so protected in these magical energies.

The heat on my face shifted. When I opened my eyes, I saw that the clouds had moved and now blocked the sunlight. That was a sign for me to get up and tune in to the land, as much as the spirits would allow. I took a deep breath and prayed. The physical sensations I'd felt earlier started to reappear. Intense heat and itching were dominant. I allowed these energies to expand so that I could be clearer about them. As I did, I remembered to call upon every voice of that land that had given me access to its light, and every plant spirit that I had been introduced to thus far. I realized why my shaman was there—to give me extra protection.

I am you and you are me; wherever you are, I am there. And I am scattered in all things; from wherever you want to you gather Me; and in gathering Me, you gather yourself.
—The Gospel of Eve

As the energies moved through me, I couldn't breathe. It felt as though my lungs were filling up with smoke and it became dark around me. I could hear screams and cries, and the earth felt like it was moving under me. Animals were scattering in confusion and disarray as I was somehow energetically being transported back to another time. The visions started to come, and I could see glimpses of the massacre that had taken place.

I had previously known that there was bloodshed in this land, but there was something unique about this particular piece of land. It was here, I realized, that the women and children had been taken and raped, abused, separated, and tortured. The women and children I now saw seemed to number in the hundreds—new faces, more than I had been allowed to observe before. The fires, many of them, and the flames were constant... it was a continual burning. All the people were suffering. At that time, it was not unusual for male warriors or tribesmen to be killed in a massacre, but for this number of women's lives to be taken was in some way abominable. And for some reason, their souls took hold of the land ... so that if they became lost in the spirit world, they could find each other here.

I somehow understood that. This land had acted as a womb to these women, the seat of power where life and death begins and ends. One of the connections they had to the earth and to what was transpiring was this piece of ground I was sitting on. How could anything grow on it now? Its soul had been taken away. The grief I felt around me was profound, and part of what the spirits wanted was recognition. But these visions and feelings were more than I'd wanted to experience. I brought myself out of my meditative space and got up quickly. I was done for the day.

I went back to the house and my friends. I told them about my visions, and they asked if there was anything they could do. My answer will always be the same to anyone who asks that question: *pray*. Simply, undeniably, inexorably pray.

I went to bed and asked for a medicine dream. Was there anything that the spirits needed me to do in my prayers, to repent for what had happened? If so, I would be open to it. Not that I thought what transpired was my fault in any way, but on an energetic level we all need to share the responsibility, just as I heard the voices tell me.

My sleep was erratic. I tossed and turned until the early hours of the morning. I had a glass of water by my bed, but it wasn't enough to quench my thirst. Lines of sweat rolled down my forehead. It felt like I was still attached to the heat I'd felt on the land—heat that was partially from those fires burning—and I would think of the cumulative anger that arose about the atrocities taking place. I was itchy again and did what I could to fall asleep. Somehow I managed to, because the next thing I knew I was dreaming.

In my dreams, I saw a gathering of Native American women dancing around a fire. There was one in particular that I noticed; she was short in stature but full-bodied. The lines of her face were drawn with character, matching her strength, wisdom, and maturity. I knew she was a healer, a medicine woman, a person of peace. She was leading the others in a tribal dance and motioning me to come and join in. She chanted, and then moved her body upward toward the sky, and then downward toward the earth, allowing her entire being to touch and merge with the earth. She offered herself and the soul of her womb to the Great Mother, cradling the ground as she searched for a peaceful energy that would come forth. As she sprang upward, branches of black cohosh appeared in her hand. She danced around the fire, touching every woman with it. She also came over to me and blessed me with it. I stayed back from the fire and the other women in my dream, since I felt uncomfortable. She spoke in a language that I couldn't understand, but the words of her prayer I heard clearly.

"O sacred grounds of the earth, lull our spirits to rest upon your divine heartbeat. Take from us our pain so that you may transform it with your profound healing energy."

They all danced that prayer, their faces entranced by the sacredness of the chant and their medicine woman. The fire glowed radiantly as, one by one, they seemed to draw near to it to give it thanks. In my mind, I asked the medicine woman if there was any way I could make an offering to the souls who had perished on that land, and to the physical land itself. I had a feeling she knew that my friends wanted to grow vegetation on it, but she did not address that issue. She showed me, through her eyes, that I should gather myself and my friends on that land and to do a ceremony. She wanted a black cohosh planted in the middle of that land with some stones around it—a sort of sanctuary. She asked for lots of prayers, and let me know that all would be present.

I woke up the next day a little excited. I ran to breakfast and told my friends to retrieve a black cohosh plant and call a few other friends up. In the afternoon, a few of us went down to the site, including a friend who facilitated sweat lodges. We all gathered in a circle and called in the spirits. We'd brought offerings, which we placed in the middle of the one-fifth acre of land along with the black cohosh. One by one, we offered prayers out loud. After the last person spoke, I went into a deeper space, allowing the visions and feelings to come once more so that we might all become one with them. I remembered the plant spirit prayer of the black cohosh, and said it aloud so that one and all could hear.

> *"O sacred grounds of the earth, lull our spirits to rest upon your divine heartbeat. Take from us our pain so that you may transform it with your profound healing energy."*

I repeated the words numerous times, and began to feel the heat rise up in my body and the itching start. The visions and physical sensations were coming more quickly this time. I recounted them aloud, so that everyone would know what I saw and heard.

Little flower, if I could understand what you are, root and all, and all in all, I should know what God is and what man is.

—Alfred, Lord Tennyson

The blaze of the fires seemed greater in this vision. The children's cries went through my bones. There was one little one, with scorch marks on his face, running with outstretched hands and screaming for his mother. He found her. There were grandmothers and grandfathers, too old and feeble to walk fast enough to escape the flames that seemed to engulf them from every direction. They did what they could to help their adult children and the little ones. The elders couldn't fight off the enemies who would torture the women and hurt the children—there were just too many of them. They tried. They fought valiantly as lives were taken. I kept looking around to find the able-bodied men of the clan, but they were few and far between. Whether they were away at war themselves or on a hunt I did not know. All I saw was the lack of protection that these souls had.

I repeated these visions over and over, along with whatever else came to me. I started to sound verbose, but I just couldn't fathom what I was seeing. When I intermittently brought myself out of the visions, I could see the astonished and guilty looks on my friends' faces. What did they have to feel guilty about? Perhaps their compassion led them to feel universally responsible, as it did for me, and it was clear by the looks on their faces that they wanted to do something. They all were starting to feel physical sensations as I talked. I kept talking until the energies—of the visions we were seeing and of the thoughts and emotions that united us as one—went through me. I could see my shaman in the ethers, holding the space for all of us.

After twenty minutes or so, the visions subsided, as did the physical feelings and emotions that we were all experiencing. We threw some tobacco on the ground, along with whatever else we brought that was holy. We adorned the black cohosh with some more natural decorations and offered our sanctuary up to the souls who were lost. It didn't seem important anymore to my friends that this land yield a harvest. The air had become cold, and we closed the space and left the spirits in peace.

I had one more day left in the mountains. I finished up my work and felt sad about leaving. I wanted to get back home, though, to attend to the plants I'd planted for my book, and I also missed my cats. The day went by quickly, and the next thing I knew my bags were packed and already in the van for the train station.

We were running late, but I wanted to say a quick good-bye to my friends of the mountains, forest, and sacred land. They knew I was coming—the spirits, I mean. I went to my usual place and hundreds of souls walked out among the trees. It really was an image to behold. They were luminous. No words were spoken, but feelings were exchanged from heart to heart. I did hear one message, though. They asked me to look down right where I was standing, because there was a present for me. Not even half a foot away from my feet was a feather. I picked up the feather and said thank you.

I waved goodbye and told them I would miss them. I ran back to the house; my friends were waiting in the van for me. I showed them the feather. One of my friends, an avid bird watcher, said it was impossible that that feather would be found in this part of the country. The bird it belonged to wasn't indigenous to the area, or even to anywhere nearby. Unfortunately, I can't recall the name of the bird. And maybe we were mistaken...

An hour into the drive to the train station, we turned on the radio and were listening to an announcer talk about the mundane. Then, in the course of his banter, he mentioned this bird out of the blue and talked about the significance of it. My friends and I just looked at one another, and the confounded looks on our faces was enough of a confirmation that the feather was truly a gift to me from the spirit world.

I keep the feather on one of my bookshelves, framed. And oh yes—a year after our ceremony, vegetation started to grow on that barren area of my friends' land.

I arrived back home after a twenty-hour ordeal on the train. I love the scenic route of the railroad... I just didn't realize how tiring it would all be.

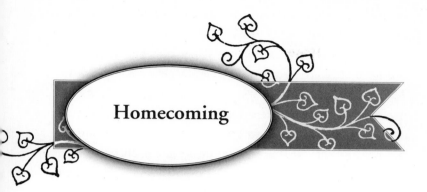

Homecoming

The first thing I wanted to do when I walked in the house was to see my cats. Ceara came up to me and greeted me as usual, and when I looked for Alexis, I spotted her in the corner. I went over to her where she huddled but she pulled away from my touch. I looked closer and saw that she had a six-inch African porcupine quill sticking out of her neck. After I called my mother in a panic, I rushed Alexis to the vet. She was incredibly lucky, but the vet kept asking me why my cat had a porcupine quill stuck in her neck. He said that the way it was jammed in, it looked as though someone had stabbed her with it.

That needle had been lying atop one of my shelves, out of sight. There was no way Alexis could get to it. I know that sometimes in our work, even though we are protected and taught to stay in the light, there are malevolent spirits who do harm. I felt that this was what happened to Alexis. During my most recent work with the plants, I had seen how animals take on our issues and protect us from harm. As I left the vet's office and took Alexis home, I saw the spirits who protected her—the Native Americans and the animal spirits and, of course, the plants. It was pretty miraculous.

I took a break for a few weeks, tending to clients and checking in on my garden. I had a lot of material already for my book, and soon would gather the plants and give them a voice too. My shaman was around again, more so than ever. It felt good to be back. Over the past few months with my clients, I'd utilized what I'd learned in a more conscious way; although I'd been working along these lines to some degree all along, the effectiveness and privileges bestowed by those above and beyond are tenfold after they initiate you into their medicine and healing world.

The kiss of the sun for pardon,
The song of the birds for mirth,
One is nearer God's heart in a garden,
Than anywhere else on earth.
—Dorothy Frances Gurney

Two weeks seemed more than enough time to rest, as far as my shaman was concerned. It was time to start gathering plants. I began to perceive that I would also make medicines, flower essences, and plant spirit remedies. A friend of mine who owned an herbal apothecary taught me how to make the medicines, and when I was working with them, the process was refined by nature and the elementals.

It was a Monday when I gathered the first leaf from the first plant that I wanted to voice. I didn't feel the need to always work with the flowers if they were in bloom; I wanted to touch the green. I wanted to feel the plant's extremities. I went into my small urban backyard on a very rainy day and just stopped at the first plant that was calling me. Calendula. *Calendula officinalis.* The flowers were indeed in bloom. I took one of them, but I decided I would work with a leaf as well. As always, I asked permission from the plant and its protectors and then put down a small gift.

Sometimes I give something sweet. The earth and its spiritual inhabitants really do have a sweet tooth!

I took the calendula flower and leaf inside and went into my living room. My candles were lit, and I think both of the cats were hanging out (they always loved being a part of my work; Ceara would come to sessions and Alexis would quietly assist me in her own way). I sat down on my red carpet and held the calendula in my hand, with my journal and pen sitting in front of me.

Just as my shaman had taught me, I tuned in to calendula and waited for its prayer.

> *"Play with me, O joyful one, and shine your radiance under the sun. Bring comfort, joy, and innocence to all, for we behold your beauty for one so small."*

I paused, then burst into prayer, feeling a beatific smile come across my face.

> *"Play with me, O joyful one, and shine your radiance under the sun. Bring comfort, joy, and innocence to all, for we behold your beauty for one so small."*

The little leaf was vibrating in my hand. My living room turned into a magical place each time I worked with a plant to channel its healing energies and medicine. It would become misty from the ethers and from the spirits who formed around me. I waited for the calendula elemental to appear. I knew my shaman was with me. Actually, a few plant gods were present. I had made many friends on my trip to the mountains and found that I had acquired new teachers in the spirit world—new medicine men and women and new plant gods—to assist me in my work. They didn't belong to me; I was still their child, wanting to learn whatever it is they wanted to teach me. My shaman and I were close—he felt more like family to me. As a child I had always loved school and wanted to become close with my teachers; it was the same now that I was an adult, only these teachers were beyond the veil. I hungered for knowledge and for their approval, and hoped that I was disciplined enough to earn whatever gems of wisdom they might bestow on me.

They were all present this day to watch me learn from the plants and their elementals. They would not interfere unless I was headed down the wrong path. I had a sense that some of them might even have been proud of me.

I called to calendula. Excitedly, a little girl appeared to me. She was surrounded by butterflies and flowers, and all of God's creatures abounded. My living room was Paradise in an instant. She was joyful. Growing near to her was an abundant amount of calendula. She became smitten with its flowers, and the magic enticed her to dance upon its soft earthen petals. Birds fluttered through the strands of yellow hair that flew from her small head. She was drunk with calendula's healing magic and made a sacred pact, the kind that only children can make, with the calendula plant. She wanted to share its medicine with every living creature under the sun.

I relished this vision for a few moments, and then my writing hand became inflamed with heat. I knew it was time to pick up my pen and journal.

> ... *The spirit of this plant is called upon to help children... it helps them feel safe in a world where they might be alone... heals the inner child... reconnects one with their lost innocence... brings laughter, creates boundaries... tonifies the thymus gland, improves cognitive function, alleviates muscle tension... an herbal oil infused with calendula is good for joint pain...*

My hand went on and on and on. I think I wrote about calendula for an hour. Then again, all of the plants took me at least that long. As each emotion passed through me, I would feel each physical ailment in my tissues, organs, muscles, and bones.

I hadn't realized it, but by the time I was finished with calendula, the leaf had withered to such an extent in my palm that it had started to fall apart. I remembered something similar happening on my trip to the mountains. I was tired after each session with a plant, but my body and mind were clearer. While the flora in the mountains belonged to the mountains, the energy was a little different with the plants I'd grown in my backyard. They had been cultivated with New York City energy and with my hard work, love, and attention. My connection with them felt more personal.

I worked with two plants each day. Some of their elementals were a little too eager to become my friends. I remember once, at about four in the morning, I was woken from a deep sleep by the spirit of dandelion flying through my room. I was saddened over the loss of a close friend and had been grieving since the week before. I woke up because someone was tickling me. Thinking I was dreaming, I went back to sleep, then was woken up again. I saw a young boy whizzing like a fairy across my bedroom, laughing gleefully and trying to play with me. I don't think he cared what time it was; he just wanted to make me smile!

The Divine Nature is simple, pure, unique, immutable, unalterable, ever abiding in the same way, and never goes outside of itself. It is utterly immune to any participation in evil and thus possesses the good without limit, because it can see no boundary to its own perfection.
—Gregory of Nyssa

Strange things were happening those weeks that I worked with the plants. My physical body remained strong, but funny things were happening around me and I knew it had to do with the plants. I would misplace things, things kept dropping, the cats were scattered. Nothing that occurred felt negative; it all just seemed so haphazard.

Dandelion was a very fun plant to work with. The morning I went into my backyard to gather its flower and leaf, I saw a stray cat who was staying around the garden throughout this time. He protected the garden, and he seemed to be protective of me. He would wait for me on my front stoop when I went out at night, and when I came home, he waited for me to go through my front door and then left. (I named him Sammie; after I finished my work with the plants, Sammie found a loving home with my mom and her dog. He is still happily enjoying himself in her abode with her other pets and of course, my mom's array of houseplants.) Sammie watched placidly as I tiptoed between the plants, seeking out the dandelion. It was actually a bit hard to find, because it was also growing all over my backyard and in the little patch of soil in front of my house. But I wanted to procure the flower and leaf from the specific plant I'd been praying over ever since I planted it.

The golden-yellow petals of its flower were so astounding that I didn't want to injure the plant at all. I bent down to it and gently placed my fingers around the stem, asking permission to take a flower and a leaf. When I felt I'd been given the go-ahead to do so, I gracefully plucked the flower and leaf. With these two living things in my hand, I went back into my living room and sat on the floor once again. Once I started to pray, it didn't take long for the mist to appear. Candles were lit, and all that I needed was placed on the floor in front of me.

"Joyful spirit, full of glee, fill me, embrace me,
and shelter me. Make this magic of the most high,
grant my dreams unto the sky."

It didn't take long for that whimsical young boy with the fairy-like energy to come flying by me. I don't think I'd even uttered the last word of the prayer. Wherever he flew, a rainbow trailed behind him. I could tell he loved rainbows, because he would look behind him after each one appeared and smile. The colors in this vision were so real that I could touch them. Even this young magical boy exuded colors— he emoted colors. When he smiled, brilliant colors appeared in his aura. He was very empathic, so if he picked up on an emotion from me, various colors appeared. That was one of his gifts. He so loved the golden yellow hues of dandelion. He sat atop some of his rainbows and showed me that he could grant wishes to people in honor of the dandelion.

The energy of the vision was halted by my hand heating up again. I began to write whatever came through.

> *... Helps with depression and sadness ... assists with grief and loss ... gives strength during a soul loss, deals with shock, sudden trauma, loss ... brings abundance and good fortune ...*
>
> *Good remedy for headaches and sinus infections ... mucus in the lungs, lowers blood pressure, increases circulation, energy surrounding diabetes ...*

I wrote until the words stopped flowing, and, as with all the other plants whose energy was channeled through me, the emotions and the physical ailments became part of me for a few moments in time. At the end of the session, as I expected, the flower and the leaf had given their life force and withered.

I spent a few days doing this each week, until I was done with the thirty plants that I'd grown in my garden. My book was coming together. I hadn't yet put anything formal into a computer—all my notes were written with pen on paper— but I was elated.

I cured with the power that came through me. Of course, it was not I who cured, it was the power from the outer world. The visions and the ceremonies had only made me like a hole through which the power could come to the two-leggeds. If I thought I was doing it myself, the hole would close up and no power could come through. Then everything I could do would be foolish.
—Black Elk

Still to come, however, were the flower essences, or remedies. Having just finished working with the plants themselves, I couldn't wait to make my thirty mother tinctures. (Mother tinctures are the first stage of a vibrational remedy, incorporating a plant, animal, or mineral substance in a mixture of water and alcohol.) I had originally intended to take a break and wait a few weeks before starting this process; I wanted to focus on my clients and invite the new spiritual energies I'd been working with into my practice. But one evening on the local news, they announced that the spraying would soon begin again. I was very angry, to say the least. The powers that be were all concerned about the West Nile Virus, yet the pesticides were what posed the greater risk.

Previously, I had called my local councilman and put in a civilian complaint letting them know that I'd gotten sick from the spraying. They said they'd never heard of such a thing; but, of course, the first time a neurotoxin was sprayed, there were so many news reports of people having reactions from it that they changed the pesticide the following year. I was concerned once again—it had taken me a while to rebalance myself and I didn't want to go through that again. I decided to take the necessary precautions and just do what I could. That also meant I had to harvest the leaves from the plants to make the remedies earlier than planned.

It rained for a few days. I hoped the rain would continue, since it would put off the aerial spraying. It soaked the ground and the plants seemed to skyrocket. At my living room table, I prepared a number of crystal glasses that had been handed down from my Italian grandmother. I filled them with water and labeled them with their respective plant names. I had the other materials in place to make the remedies: I'd ordered the tincture bottles weeks beforehand, and I'd collected a few plant leaves at a time. I used very few blossoms for the mother tinctures—I was called to mostly use the leaves. I placed the leaves, one by one, in their coordinating crystal glasses, and when all of the thirty plants were floating atop the water in each glass, the work of making the remedy begun.

I prayed, I chanted. I used all the plant spirit prayers that had been given to me by the spirits and elementals of the natural world. I lit candles and let the glow of the candlelight surround them. The next day was supposed to be bright and sunny, so I was hoping to leave them overnight, embraced by the gentle energies of the heavens, and then place them in the early morning sunlight to be blessed.

I couldn't have asked for a better day when I woke up. Still in my pajamas, I ran into the living room, retrieved the crystal glasses two at a time, and went into my garden to place them in the walkway. Sammie, my outdoor stray, was watching as usual. My intention was to leave the glasses in the sunlight for an hour, and then begin to make and bottle the tinctures. I sat next to Sammie as all the glasses glistened in the sunlight. The leaves, interestingly enough, were not withered; they still had life to them. And I could tell that the energy of the water inside each glass was different. I prayed and asked all of nature to bless these remedies. When the time came, I made each tincture with such gratitude for the medicine I was honored to work with.

So much had happened over the last few months. I tried to piece together my destiny, as it were—the miasm, my mother's gifts, my gifts. My mom always said that before I was born she was told she was going to have a daughter who would write books and help people. I had lived a lifetime in the past year, and putting my book together would be my way of honoring not only the spirits and their teachings, but my family ancestry.

I settled in, in preparation for the chemical spraying that would start in a few days. I felt that I was more physically prepared than last time, and stronger on all levels. And with what felt like most of the miasm cleared, I hoped I would respond differently to the pesticides. But I didn't expect what happened next.

It was an excruciatingly hot day when the helicopters hovered and released their poisons. I closed all the windows, shut off the air conditioner, and planned not to leave the house until hours after it was over. The local department of environmental protection actually recommended that anyone with allergies or who was immunosuppressed stay indoors.

I had lots of work to do, so that wasn't an issue. The spraying started early in the morning, but it wasn't until dusk that they came to spray the areas close to me. I live near the water, and when there is a gentle breeze, you can feel and smell the pesticides intensify as they come your way.

The day passed and I distracted myself. I wanted it to be just another day; I stayed positive about any reaction I might have. Evening came. I cooked dinner and kept myself occupied until bedtime. Morning arrived, and I felt secure enough to venture out into the neighborhood and take care of some errands before my work started. My sense of smell is so sensitive that I could indeed smell the toxins as I walked out of my house. (Friends told me their allergies were heightened, and sensitive clients had reacted to the pesticide as well.) Over the next few days, I started getting headaches and my face took on a yellowish color, and I knew that my thyroid was affected once again. The effects weren't as intense as with the last round of spraying, but I still did not want to have to deal with them.

I'd heard about an urban shaman who practiced fifteen minutes away from me. I had never gone to her before, but decided to give something different a try. I called for an appointment and got one rather quickly. I felt a bit like we were kindred spirits when we met. I could hear the spirits talking over her, suggesting remedies for me—one of them was for detoxing and one of them was for spiritual protection. She said I needed both. But I was disoriented that day due to the headache and light-headedness, and I didn't correctly write down everything she told me to do. She was from one of the islands in the Caribbean, and the herbs she suggested were indigenous to that region, so I wasn't acquainted with them.

I left my appointment feeling reassured that along with my continued methods of healing, the medicinals and suggestions this urban shaman made would clear me of this pesticide residue once and for all. After this spraying, I had a sense that my reactions each time would be lessened. I would turn out to be right.

I waited a few days before starting the remedies. The effects of the sprays were continuing to work their way through my body, and I paid close attention to eating the right foods and cleansing. My sleep patterns were very much changed and my senses were extremely heightened. I felt, once again, more "open" than usual and didn't want to be in large crowds. I also found myself reacting to things I had never reacted to before. This was something new, and didn't occur with the last round of spraying. I became sensitive to foods that I'd tolerated previously; lotions, creams, and even things made with the purest of ingredients made my body feel uncomfortable. I was having what felt like an all-over allergy response. The usual burning and swelling up of various parts of my body occurred, and

I was getting frustrated at the thought of this happening all over again.

I finally started using the two remedies the shaman had given me, setting aside things I was already taking so that I could feel the effects of these medicinals alone. I made a tea out of both herbs. I was to drink two cups a day of the one she'd given me to detox my body. The other was from a bush, and she'd given me a pound of the roots. It was used in her native home to protect oneself from malevolent spirits. When we'd met, however, I'd grossly misunderstood her and thought she'd suggested that I drink five to eight cups a day of this root. What she actually suggested was that I take five to eight sips throughout the day, since this is a toxic substance if taken in higher doses. I drank five cups that first day!

Well, after the first few cups, I was so energized that I wanted to know all I could about the herb I was taking. I couldn't find anything, given the slang name the shaman had given me. I trusted her, and figured I would come across it within the next few days, so I wasn't concerned. My body was feeling stronger, so I thought it was working.

I continued to drink, and over the next three days upped the dosage by a cup or two. By day three I was so euphoric that I wasn't sleeping at all. I'd visited my acupuncturist for a session and he'd remarked that he'd never seen my pulses like that. He said they didn't feel like my pulses and that they were all pretty good. He was curious about what I was taking, but he wasn't himself familiar with the plant.

I went home and figured all was good. By day four, I noticed that my cat Alexis was sleeping on me, specifically on my abdomen right over my liver. My high had ended, and over the next few days I lowered the dosage for some reason and started to crash. I needed to rest in between work and each time, Alexis would sit on top of me and sleep on my liver. By day six, I had stopped taking the medicinal and went online to find this plant. By the grace of God I came upon it and saw that it was in the same family as mistletoe. My mouth dropped open, since as I knew how toxic this herb was, and I called the urban shaman immediately. When I told her how much I had been consuming, she gasped and said she had ever heard of anyone even able to consume that much without serious harm being done.

I made an appointment the next day with my internist and told him what had happened. He just looked at me, stunned, and did all the necessary tests to make sure I didn't have liver damage and that my heart was functioning normally. He took some blood for testing, and to our surprise, I was not affected at all by the overdose. Everyone who knew what had transpired was amazed. I was just grateful, and felt so stupid that I misheard the instructions.

I spent the next month detoxing from both the medicinal and the pesticide. Even though it was a toxic dose, it had seemed to do the trick. My cleansing was pretty cathartic, and my body became stronger than it had been before and the pesticides came out faster than they did in the last round of spraying. Each night, Alexis would sleep on me in the same area, giving me comfort as my body burned and sweated out the poisons.

Time went by, and I knew things were clearing up. Alexis also went back to her usual sleeping space on one of the many pillows next to me. I remember thinking one day that she looked great because she had gained a little weight, but then the weight kept coming and I knew something wasn't right.

The important thing is that the mythic vision lead to a sustainable context for the survival and continued evolution of the Earth and its living forms.
—Thomas Berry

I made an appointment with my vet. I wasn't concerned, and thought maybe her thyroid was out of balance. She'd helped me through my cleansing, and for sure it had affected her somehow. When the vet came in to examine her, he saw her stomach distended and wanted to get some X-rays. It was at that point that I said to myself, "Alexis has liver cancer." The vet came back into the room after about a half hour and told me the news. Most likely it was cancer, but it needed to be confirmed with an ultrasound.

Words cannot express what was going through my mind. The vet drained the fluids out of Alexis' abdomen to make her more comfortable, and we came back a few days later for the ultrasound. My fears were confirmed and Alexis was diagnosed with hepatic cancer. The vet said her prognosis was grim and that surgery would not be useful in this case, nor chemotherapy. The fluids would continuously build up in her abdomen and then possibly her lungs, causing suffocation. They needed to be drained every few days, so I asked the vet to show me how. I did this with Alexis at home.

I brought Alexis back home from that appointment and just looked at her. That was why she had been lying on my liver all those nights. That was why my tests had come out okay. She'd taken the side effects of the medicinals from me. Was it supposed to happen like this? With all the work I'd just done with the plant elementals and the plant gods, weren't they going to save her?

I was angry. I was angry with the spirit world, with God, with myself, with the shaman. I was angry at everyone and everything. I was in shock and couldn't accept that within a month or so, I would lose something so precious to me.

I stayed up late that night. I took out my rosary and prayed really hard. When I finished with my novenas, I prayed to the plant gods. Then I prayed to the elementals. I prayed and asked every spirit that I'd met over the past year to save the life of my cat.

The days went by slowly during her decline. Alexis was able to walk and eat and play for those first two weeks after her diagnosis, so I thought maybe she could be cured. Every day I called upon a different plant, one that had grown in the garden. I called upon black cohosh and feverfew. I prayed to motherwort and blessed thistle. I chanted the prayers to clematis and violet. And one by one, they all came and surrounded her. I remember clearly the day Alexis was sitting on my sofa and I saw the Native American spirits talking to her. Her ears were pointed upward as if she was listening. I still thought for sure a miracle would happen. How could it not, with all these spirits coming to help her?

By the third week, Alexis grew weak and weary. She wasn't able to walk well, so I would bring food to where she lay. She couldn't jump up on the bed to sleep with me, so I put up steps for her to climb. I started to think that a miracle wasn't going to happen, that the spirits didn't listen to my prayers. She started having pain in her right front paw and she would stick her paw into her drinking bowl to cool it off. I kept asking her if it was time for her to go and if so, it would be okay. If she needed assistance, she should just let me know. But she was a fighter and I realized that the time was near, but not yet.

Over a weekend, the signs became clearer. Alexis stopped coming near me and slept in the living room. She lost most of her appetite and was nursing the paw that hurt her. Spirits that I hadn't seen in a while started to appear. My shaman was constantly around and loved Alexis. John, the soul from the cemetery, was around. The lost children were around. And some of the spirits I had befriended from my trip to the mountains were around. I didn't have the emotional energy to tune in to why they were there, since I was so despondent over Alexis. The house was becoming cold, despite the warmth of the energy those spirits brought. Eventually, I couldn't ignore them any longer and wanted to understand why they were here. I knew Alexis had taken on my stuff. Were there other reasons that this had happened?

Apparently there were. The residual energies of the miasm needed to complete themselves. Sometimes, when an ancestral pattern is this big and has a lot of karma attached to it, there is a die-off reaction, so to speak. Something in physical form has to return to where it came from. It doesn't always mean a physical death, but there is a death on many levels that has to occur for completion—and sometimes, unfortunately, in the physical realm as well. Alexis had lovingly offered to assist me with bringing this miasm to completion. She took on the residuals of the pesticides and the medicinals which were lodged in my liver and lymph glands, as well as the energy of the many spirits that were still stuck in my energy field and needed to cross over. They couldn't cross until something else was sacrificed and another piece of spiritual work was complete. There were some of the lost children who were frightened to cross over, and the soul of a beloved pet seemed to comfort their fears.

Do not treat lightly the things that enter a person's life. Receive them for what they are and then try to make them fit tools for enlightenment.
—Lord Buddha

Alexis also held onto things that I had been carrying for the last fifteen years, and it was time for her to let them go. It was time for my body to be given a different boundary with these ancestors and to purge some of their weaknesses. Alexis knew that. I wasn't ready for her to go, but she knew it was time. John, the soul from the cemetery, came to bring me comfort and support, and to assure me that Alexis would be okay. In fact, it seemed as if all the spirits who were present knew of this beforehand; it seemed like they were all waiting for her. I was continually reassured that Alexis would be okay with her transition and that she would be able to see me and her sister Ceara when she crossed. She would be able to visit and play any time she wanted.

It seemed as if I had no choice. There was no bargaining here, and destiny was at play. All were eagerly waiting for her to cross.

The day came, and Alexis cried a cry that I had never heard. She looked at me to say goodbye, but she had trouble dying. I told her it would be okay and brought her to the vet to be euthanized. We had had animals all our lives growing up, but I had never been with one when we had to put them to sleep.

That night was one of the saddest I could remember in a long time. I had lost an animal companion. More than that—she had saved my life, even more than I realized. When I came home from the vet and walked into my living room, I saw all the spirits dancing. I wasn't happy, so I obviously didn't join in. I sat on my bed crying, and felt a cat jump on the bed behind me. I thought it was Ceara coming to comfort me but when I turned around, I saw indentations going onto the pillow near where I put my head to sleep—and no physical cat there. I stared in disbelief. At that moment, Ceara jumped onto the bed and sat next to me. We both just stared at the pillow without moving. We knew Alexis was with us, lying on her pillow. All was well.

I slept that night. I slept long and hard. When I awoke, life was different. Something had stilled itself within me and around me.

After that night, I never really saw John again. Every once in a while, one of the lost children might appear. The spirits I met in the mountains don't come around anymore. The plant elementals come when I call to them, and my shaman—well, he is always there when I need him. Alexis hangs around me often. She actually was around me as I wrote this book, and was present when her sister Ceara was diagnosed with heart failure. My shaman and all those in heaven knew beforehand that Ceara would take ill. They also knew that I would be calling on the plant spirits.

A lot of miracles happened when Alexis crossed over. She was given life, a life beyond the veil without suffering. The miasm no longer holds any power over me, and I was initiated into the spiritual world of plants and plant gods. I was accepted as one of their own, still low on the totem pole, but granted privileges within their world. My body had shifted. I have very little reaction each year when they spray the pesticides. Changes also took place within my immediate family. Looking back, it all sometimes seems like a dream, but when I hear those footsteps behind me in the ethers, I know that my shaman still walks behind me. I'm blessed to share in a world where miracles really do happen, and where the natural world is a big part of that!

The Divine Nature of Plants

My work with the plants themselves was a humbling experience. Besides the emotional and spiritual curative properties that are present in a plant, there is the very real physical form of a plant. The color, the texture, the shape, the size of each petal on every blossom, the intricacy of the roots, the simplistic beauty. Never take for granted what nature can give you.

Plants have a voice. They perhaps have many voices. In the following pages, I hope you will hear and feel this beauty as I have. I hope you will embrace the healing that they offer!

Human Beings and the Plant Kingdom

I believe that the essence of humankind, and each individual's birthright, stems from God like the leaves of the many flowers, plants, and trees of creation. In the manifestation of a living thing, the miracle of grace showers its spiritual energy into the earth plane, harvesting fruit of the divine womb. The seedlings and flowers the plant bears represent our many aspirations toward the Divine. In our search for meaning, our relationship to God has been marked by his relationship with the earth and all of its creatures. We may find it easier to communicate with the living things of God than with the Creator him/herself. In connecting with the many plants and flowers, we find the mystical aspect of the Divine grounded in a way that resembles the physicality of our own survival on earth.

In this way, we mirror the plant—in its earth form as self, and in the divine form as god and goddess. The earth form of a plant shares the same characteristics that we do. It begins as a seed, like an embryo in the womb. Through nourishment, the seed grows and matures and is able to walk its own path. It needs sunlight, food, appropriate shelter, and love. It is nourished by respect, appreciation, and acknowledgment. Within the essence of the plant, as within us, are the mysteries of God. The plant's innate spiritual and medicinal healing abilities are forthright and honored as part of its core. Its spiritual connection to the Divine, to the God within, is apparent; the soul line of a plant stems from deep within the earth and reaches far into the heavens. We, as humans, are nourished from the moment we enter our mother's wombs, but our spirits are nourished even before then. With tender loving encouragement, we are given the tools to walk this path in life; our soul line also stems from deep within the earth and reaches far into the heavens. But we have hidden ourselves behind veils of tears and shadows, afraid to shine in the image and

From Wankan Tanka, the Great Mystery, comes all power. It is from Wankan Tanka that the holy man has wisdom and the power to heal and make holy charms. Man knows that all healing plants are given by Wankan Tanka, therefore they are holy.
—Flat Iron, Oglala Sioux Chief

likeness of the Divine that is inherent within each one of us. The plants have much to teach us.

Each and every plant maintains a level of responsibility for the earth and its inhabitants; it holds the space for evolutionary growth. In so doing, plants show us the road that leads to the kingdom of God. Their stems represent our grounding, our connection to Mother Earth, the placenta that nourished us inside the womb and still energetically and spiritually nurtures us through life. The stem is that part of the plant that sustains it, that part which feeds us physically and holds the space for us to find our way back to Spirit—within, above, and beyond. The sepals of the plant (the leaves the encase the gentle bud) protect the bud until it can open and expand itself to receive the complete blessings of the Divine. Likewise, in choosing to live as human beings and learning to love, the outer shell we carry serves as our protection.

Remembering that all things turn to dust and eventually return to the earth, the spirit always returns home. Following the way of grace is the route that both plants and humans take. Grace is that miracle in life where the energies of God meet the energies of humanity. Within that realm the circle of life begins, as does the journey back to our essence. We call on grace to nourish our souls and help us to clear the road ahead. In working with plants, never underestimate their connection to God. They utilize God's sacred power to bring joy, beauty, and healing into the world.

Like us, plants have aspirations, represented by their many petals and leaves. Petals are similar to the many layers of the human energy field, and the various levels of evolution and enlightenment. There are many paths that lead to Spirit, and each one has a different story to tell, a different lesson to teach. On each path, there are physical, emotional, and spiritual relationships that are created so that we can

serve our highest purpose. Each of the petals of a plant resonates with a part of a life story, and with a vibrational frequency of light that is needed for healing. The plant's work
on the earth plane is to make the connection between the
earth story and the light; this is our work as well. The sepals
we carry are reminders and guides that escort us through
life and back to the light, which never left us.

Each plant is imbued with the feminine and the masculine aspects of the Divine, which are learning to be in relationship with each other. It is the honoring and integration
of each of these aspects that brings unity to the plant's life
force. This unity gives the plant strength to move and grow
in the direction of God, and a purpose for fulfilling its mission. The life force of the whole plant can deliver the grace
of Spirit to itself, to the earth, and to many of us.

The interrelationships in the plant kingdom signify the
interrelationships we have among the many different cultures here on earth, and the many faces of God. That is the
beauty of life. All of the living creatures that come from love
are unique in their own forms. Although unique, we are all
still one and connected with tiny strands of light, each of
which breathes fire and air into the collective consciousness.
We strive to work together to heal humanity, and each kingdom—be it animal, mineral, or plant—serves Spirit in the
same capacity. Truth follows energy. Energy follows love.
Love follows oneness. In maintaining the truth that we are
all one, we become part of the plant world and receive as
many teachings as our consciousness will allow.

My intention in this work is to bring you some of those
teachings. The evolution of plants is not a mystery; it is we
who create the illusion of mystery. The plants exist to teach
us. They are like enlightened beings who choose to forego
Nirvana in order to remain here and teach us the Way—and
their way is one of humility, simplicity, and eternal truth.

Most plants have markings on their leaves, petals, or stems that show us the many times we humans have forgotten the truth. In a way, they bear the scars and joys of human evolution. They still choose to thrive and give love when we ask for it. While serving Spirit, they remain humble in their teachings and continue to offer us new ways to heal.

This whole new world of healing is open to us—the spirit, leaves, roots, flowers, and other parts of a plant can be transformed into medicines to heal the various different levels of our being. Plants can heal vibrationally, since our spirits work in mirrored relationship to those of the plant kingdom; when we need assistance on the physical, emotional, mental, or spiritual levels, the plant can access different healing states of consciousness in order to produce the right remedies for us. These remedies work in conjunction with the desired healing intent, while simultaneously effecting healing in other parts of ourselves. For example, if you have lung congestion, the plant will harvest a remedy not only for the lungs, but also for the emotional and spiritual issues that are related to the physical malady. The beauty of this method is that most of the plants willingly share this information. All one has to do is ask.

The Plant's Soul

Each plant is like the nectar of the Divine, and has a soul just as we do. Its soul is three-dimensional, and the realm of the soul unfolds as such. The lower part of the plant's soul is the plant itself in physical form. Its higher soul is the Godself. The middle way of the plant's soul is the realm of the plant spirits and devas, the many beings who help to activate the miraculous healing abilities of the plant kingdom. When working with the plant, we are truly working with its soul. Just as we need our soul to breathe in life, plants need soul to sustain themselves.

The plant spirits are very interesting, in that they maintain some sort of personality within their working dimensions. Plant spirits may appear as animals, beings, symbols, and many other things. These are the beings we call on and rely upon for assistance. Each spirit resonates at the same frequency as the plant and also serves as its protector. These spirits are messengers between worlds, dimensions, and realities. They bring our prayers from the earth level to the Divine to be heard and answered. In forming a relationship with plants, we form a relationship with Spirit. The plant kingdom is a very safe way to open doors into that world. When we heal at the human level, we are always working with Spirit. In working with plants, it is the same. When our prayers are answered, grace at the earth level is working divinely in our lives.

Each plant spirit has something to share with us about the world and how we have evolved as a healing species. When we explore plant spirits, we acknowledge their gifts to our growth as a whole, and also work in communion with them to continue to heal ourselves. As we heal ourselves, we heal each other. What reflects within, reflects without.

Thus the sage knows without traveling; the sage sees without looking; the sage works without doing.
—Lao Tzu

In healing each other, we heal the earth and all the manifestations of God. This, of course, makes all the plant spirits very happy. We learn to respect Mother Nature, and the law of reciprocity comes into being. "Do unto others as you would like to have them do unto you." This rings true for the plant kingdom as well.

We create beliefs and untruths about who we are and how we are supposed to live. When we begin working with plant spirits, our untruths become clearer, as does the Way. In all of our relationships on the earth, we strive to know ourselves and Spirit. The next time you look at a plant, try to tune in to the force that watches over it and nourishes it.

The Healing Process

Years before I started my work with the plant gods, I had my first encounter with plant spirit healing and medicine. I was a novice back then, and couldn't fully appreciate the exchange that occurred until later on.

It was many years ago, in the late evening, and I was walking with a friend in her garden. I glanced over at a plant that caught my attention. The energy around it was radiant, and its light permeated the other plants that surrounded it. I walked over to it and asked my friend what it was. "Lamb's ear," she said. I knew by the vibration and light that lamb's ear had something special to share. I didn't know anything about the plant, but just by tuning in to it, a story began to unfold for me. I started receiving impressions about its spiritual healing qualities, and I knew I needed to tincture the healing properties into an essence. My friend graciously showed me how. (Later on, I learned from another friend how to make flower essences, and then I learned on my own.)

When I gave thanks to the plant for sharing its medicine, three fireflies came fluttering around me, acknowledging the exchange. That night was the first time that I became curious about the spiritual essence of a plant. Some of what I have written below stems from my thoughts on that summer evening.

In working with plants to effect healing, we are working with two interrelated aspects—the vibration and the spirit of the plant. When we call upon the spirit, we immediately come into divine relationship with the plant kingdom, and the powers of the spirit that are manifest in the healing properties of the plant. The spirit gives the plant its medicinal qualities, and will also share with you the ways and times of optimal harvesting and healing. Each spirit also has a vibration, which filters through the physical plant body and emanates outward. The physical plant graciously accepts its path and the work ahead, and embodies the healing energies of the spirit. Its vibration also resonates with the emotional, physical, and spiritual aspects of the person it will assist in the healing process. When you need healing from a plant, just listen, and the right plant will show itself.

Plant spirit healing works with light energy; it is a vibrational healing process. Each living thing is made up of light of many frequencies or vibrations. Denser vibrations become manifest in form and matter. The light around living things has different layers within it, which are qualities that resonate with the various dimensions of our spirits. One layer will resonate with the physical body, another will resonate with the emotional body, and so on. The layers are all interconnected, and one layer cannot be affected without affecting the others, as one bodily dimension cannot be healed without healing the others. In working with one layer, the vibrational healing will spread to the other ones. When we work with plants, or with the medicines that come from them, we are opening ourselves up to the vibrational healing that directs itself to the place we need it most.

Given all this, it is not surprising that working with a physical plant is not necessary for doing plant spirit medicine. Since we are engaging with Spirit and its vibration, many times we can just call on a plant's spirit to hear our prayers. Also, we can meditate or journey with a plant and obtain its healing graces without taking its medicine internally. (I only recommend taking medicines internally if the energy of the illness has permeated the tissues and cells of your body.)

Preparing for the Journey

Upon starting your journey into the world of plant spirit healing, make sure you are in a comfortable space. Whether it is a place in nature or in your own living room, gather all the tools you need to feel safe and ready for your meditation. Your tools might include music, a cushion to sit on, a drum or rattle, a notebook for recording your thoughts, some prayers, an offering of gratitude, and the plant spirit with whom you want to get acquainted. Sound is very useful, in that it can take you more easily into altered states of consciousness.

Begin with an invocation prayer. Offer the journey in light of the highest good, and thank Spirit for its willingness to participate. Always call on your teachers for assistance and protection, whatever your tradition or path. Also, keep in mind that when you travel into the spirit world there are certain things you need to be aware of, and protection is necessary. Protection may come from prayer, burning an herb or resin such as sage or copal, or from a ritual or blessing. When I do this work, I call on my guiding teachers in the spirit world. In exploring your spiritual work and inner process, always call on beings with whom you resonate and feel safe. I feel that because I'm working with a living creation of the earth, it is customary to honor the earth, its traditions, and its spiritual energies. Calling in the four elements of air, fire, water, and earth respects our connection to the Mother.

I grieve not for what I have lost, but rather for what I thought I had.
A wider more expansive vision was presented only to be withdrawn.
Leaving me with neither who I was nor who I am to be.

—Jon Dunnavent

After your guides and teachers are present, you may ask the plant spirit with whom you would like to work to become present. It is not necessary for you to have the plant with you in physical form, although working next to it is very magical and powerful. A vision of the plant will do as well. It might take a while for the plant spirit to make itself known. Like all spirits of the light, they want to make sure your intention is clear. Tell the spirit you request its presence for healing purposes and are honored by its willingness to be with you. If you have the plant within your reach, ask to touch a part of it and begin to feel its physical characteristics. If you are holding a vision, look closely at the different parts of the plant. See if you can "feel" it with your vision. Notice the texture and the shape of the leaves. Look for flowers. Hold the stem gently. Get a feel for the physicality of the plant structure and see how it mirrors the human body. The closer you get to becoming one with the plant, the sooner the plant spirit will identify itself. Once you feel a presence, you may begin your work.

If you are familiar with journeying and working in the spirit world, the spirit might come to you more readily. As you embody the physicality and energetics of the plant matrix, become aware of the sensations in your body. Notice what parts of you—organs, bones, tissues, and muscles—are experiencing different sensations. When you are in physical energetic resonance, your body begins to mirror the maladies that the plant spirit heals. Then journey deeper. Ask the plant what parts of its physicality will help to heal those sensations you are experiencing. You might be surprised at what you hear. You will receive information on how to bring the spirit of the plant into your body. This is a good time to record some of your thoughts. Thank the plant for teaching you about how it physically heals, and ask it to now help you tune in to your emotional body.

Clear your body of the physical sensations and tune in to your emotional being. Begin by gently breathing into your lower abdomen. Breathe in through your nose and exhale through your mouth. Do this a number of times to bring your consciousness into another state of awareness. Let your emotions be safely present within you, in order to bring awareness to that part of yourself you are working with. Greet your emotions and let them move through you, so that you become a clear channel in which the plant spirit can share its emotional healing qualities with you.

When you are ready, ask the plant spirit to tell you how the plant can heal your emotional body. Tune in to yourself as you do this. You will begin to notice emotions surfacing in your body. They may be the same ones as before, or different ones. They may be new. Are you experiencing grief, joy, anger, forgiveness? What healing qualities does this plant and spirit offer you? Remember that each plant will offer something different to everyone. One plant may heal grief in one person but heal anger in another. Each spirit adapts itself to the environment and to the person with whom it is communicating.

When you feel complete with the emotional healing experience, thank the plant spirit once again for its guidance. As before, clear your body by breathing into your lower abdomen, breathing in through your nose and exhaling through your mouth, and honoring and detaching from all that is moving through you at the moment so that you become a clear channel once again.

When you are ready, tune in to your spirit. Envision yourself as a ball of light, endlessly flowing out into the universe, connecting with all things, radiating loving kindness to the earth and all of her creatures. Feel your soul line stemming from deep within the earth and reaching far into the heavens. Know that you are one with the Divine. When you have come to that place, ask the plant and spirit to share with you their spiritual healing qualities. How can they help you heal your life on the spiritual level? How can they help you find or rekindle your connection to God? Listen to what the spirit tells you. You will begin to notice higher vibrations of spiritual energy working through and around you. You will begin to feel healing on a different level. Take as much time as you need with yourself in this place. The spirit and plant are healing your spirit, which, in turn, will heal your physical and emotional bodies.

When you are done with this part, acknowledge the spirit and the plant. If you haven't already seen the plant spirit clearly, ask for it to make itself known to you, if that is in alignment with the highest will. If the spirit feels it would serve you, you will make its visual acquaintance. Be patient. As on the human level, some spirits need to create a resonance of trust before showing themselves.

You have now finished journeying, and it is time to come to a completion and a letting go. I like to offer a prayer of thanks. Saying a simple thank you from the heart, or a prayer of gratitude in the tradition that you resonate with, works wonderfully. Thank the spirit of the plant and the plant itself for joining you. Also thank your guides and teachers for protecting and guiding this journey. Part of giving thanks is to make an offering. An offering is something from the heart, be it prayer, thanks, or praise to the spirit keepers and creations of the earth. You might use something from your person, like a strand of hair, or bury something sentimental that belongs to you. You might want to burn incense or resin again. The earth likes sweet-tasting things also.

After your offering, bring your awareness back to your being. I encourage you to write down some notes about your journey, and I hope you enjoy your adventure!

The Healing Dimensions

The beauty of plant spirit healing and medicine is that the plant and its elementals will focus on the dimension where healing is needed most. Even if we can't see the origin of an imbalance, it is not a problem; knowing the origin is not necessary if we have faith in the power of the plant world and its magicians.

I worked with a woman who came to see me while she was very sick. She was thirty years of age, with a history of environmental illness and energy sensitivity. She had an infection that had run a course through the urinary tract, the intestines, and the rectum, and had left her with a fever for over two months. She had difficulty breathing and walking. The doctors couldn't find very much, and she was exploring many different pathways to healing.

As we began our work together, the sacred space that we created was filled with shamans and medicine people from the outer planes. They came to share with me some of the reasons for her illness. We were transported to another lifetime, where the shamans showed me that this woman had suffered from a severe case of tuberculosis and parasitic infection. Her legs had boils on them and were bleeding from the infection, and she was ridden with fever and dementia. She was being helped by indigenous healers and friends around her. From the looks of things, though, she wasn't faring so well.

Nature is the best medicine.
—Hippocrates

The energy pattern set up in that former incarnation had stayed with my client in this lifetime and embedded itself into her energy field. Through different experiences in this lifetime, the old energy matrix became stronger and intruded into her physical body. Some of her karmic issues from this pattern became obvious, as did the emotional healing that needed to take place regarding that former life.

In order to help heal the energy around her current physical illness, we had to work energetically and spiritually to heal the karma from the past life. After the shamans showed me her previous experience, they worked with the plant spirits to heal her in her past incarnation. As my client rested quietly, they offered special prayers to invoke the help of the spirits of the medicines they planned to use. They crushed the leaves of a plant into tiny pieces in a bowl, then boiled the leaves in water to make a tea. They also spread some of the leaves over the woman's boils. The shamans continually prayed to the plant spirits during this, asking for the medicine to work.

When the tea was ready, they drank it and then spit it over the woman's body three times, drenching her from head to toe. They seemed to use this method whenever serious illness was present. Then they gently raised her head so she could sip some tea from the bowl, to help cast out any internal demons. They waved their hands over the woman's body in a fanlike manner, as though waving the energy of the illness off the body, and continued with their prayers to the plant spirits. Cloths were laid on the woman's head and body to bring down her fever and cool her from the heat of the infection, drawing out many toxins.

The shamans took about fifteen minutes to do this healing procedure. My client began to experience different sensations in her body in this reality, while the shamans were working in the other. I began to notice energies clearing off both of her bodies—in that incarnation and in the present. When the work was complete, both beings were more peaceful. The shamans closed their healing with prayers of gratitude, as I offered my own to those who had come to help. My client noticed a big shift in her present body, and felt the weight she'd carried for a long time lift off her. Her body and spirit then began to heal on a different level.

I share this story to illustrate the powerful effects of using plant spirits and their medicines to heal illness that originates at the spiritual level. Sometimes the origin of a condition may be in another incarnation, but the condition affects your present-day reality.

The plant spirits can effect change within spiritual, emotional, and physical states of being. All of our unhealed thoughts, emotions, experiences, incarnations, and karma are carried in our energy fields until the vibration is cleared with our continued personal evolution. We clear away stagnant energies by transmuting them into the higher vibrational source from which they came. When patterns stay in the energy field for lifetimes, they can cause a number of imbalances within us. Purification happens when the energies become transmuted and we grow closer in alignment to the Source.

A few years ago, I assisted on a case where a young woman was going through a lot of emotional upheaval. The practitioner working with this young woman was having some challenges with her personality. I asked permission to try to "tune in" and see what was happening in the woman's energy consciousness. I was able to see that she had suffered much sexual trauma and neglect during her childhood. As an adult, she was stuck in a pattern of identifying with abuse and abandonment and testing others to make sure they wouldn't leave her. Also in her field were many entities who were feeding upon her self-inflicted patterns of emotional abuse. What was transpiring between client and practitioner was that the entities were attacking both the practitioner and the client during the work, so it was difficult for the client to put the entities into perspective and let them go.

This situation was also testing the practitioner's own boundaries regarding his need for the client to take responsibility for herself at whatever level she could. Every time the practitioner found himself trying to affirm his boundaries and work with his client, the entities only seemed to get stronger, furthered by the client's own need to emotionally put herself down.

I suggested to the practitioner, as it came to me, to call upon the spirit of black cohosh. I explained to him how this plant spirit could energetically align with the physical, emotional, and spiritual challenges that faced his client and how it might not only help the entities find the light, but also might bring some peace of mind to his client.

Sometime later, the practitioner called to thank me, letting me know that when he called upon the black cohosh plant spirit, the entities left his client's energy field and a

The finest grace that can be asked on behalf of those who aspire to the spiritual life is an increase in heavenly light. This is a light which cannot be acquired by prolonged study or through human teaching, but which is directly infused by God. When the righteous soul obtains this light, it comes to know and love its God and eternal things in its meditations with extreme clarity and relish… It is nothing but a light of faith.

—Padre Pio

great healing session resulted. Black cohosh is excellent in assisting with trauma of this kind and I would recommend it for similar cases, both calling upon the spirit and using an essence of the plant homeopathically.

In the second half of this book, which presents the thirty plants I worked with, each plant is given a section devoted to its spiritual and emotional healing properties. Every plant has vibrational qualities that resonate with the vibrations of different emotions; when you call on a particular plant spirit to work with an emotion, its healing vibration will match the emotion, and the positive and negative poles will neutralize each other. In simple terms, light will dissipate the darkness and peace will find its way within you. The plant spirit will only work to strengthen what you already have.

When spiritual issues arise in a person's energy body, the plant spirit accesses the energies of its higher self to resonate with the one in need of healing. Your energy body, or energy field, is similar to the aura; it is an energy matrix that defines your spiritual, mental, emotional, and physical attributes. Spiritual issues may include karmic patterns, negative spirits in the energy field, "curses," and so on. Those issues are addressed at the heart-and-soul level, and the plant surrenders much of its physical body when working under these circumstances. The light from the plant spirit filters into the soul line of the person and permeates from the center outward, affecting the various layers of the energy field. It creates a solid formation, similar to a healing grid, and holds the template in place until all that needs to happen for the person happens. This is all in accordance with the will of the highest good.

Imbalances in your physical body manifest first in your energy field. In response to challenges, lifetime experiences, and holding patterns in the etheric body, illnesses arise as a means of signaling the unconscious to awaken. (The etheric body is the first layer of the energy body, and extends from the physical body; it is composed of energy upon which the physical body is based. The etheric body connects our higher forms of consciousness to our physical realities.) When a plant spirit works vibrationally to heal the physical body, it becomes denser in energy and strengthens its own field to be able to work at this level. Its own cells and tissues become imbued with nutrients that manifest from Spirit. The energies of these nutrients surround the energy field of the plant, and create an energetic transfusion into the person receiving the healing medicine.

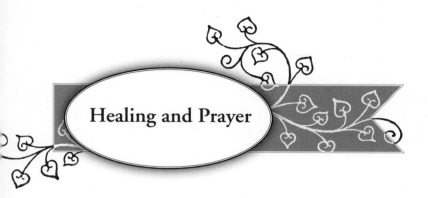

Healing and Prayer

When we heal with plant spirits, commitment to our evolution is of the utmost importance. The healings work as much as we allow them to, and insofar as we have faith. Faith is the ingredient necessary for all graces to ground themselves in physical reality. We need a willingness to explore our realities, and to look deeply within ourselves to find the original sources of our wounding. The journey requires gentleness, compassion toward oneself, non-judgment, and the ability to let go. When we surrender to the process, a miraculous partnership begins to unfold between ourselves and the world of plant spirits.

In this new partnership, the plant and its spirit form energetic bonds of light with you. Your energies become merged, and the plant spirit helps the plant adapt to your vibration and assists you in receiving the plant. The partnership is a very nurturing one, since the plant senses your healing needs on all levels. Sometimes the plant may take on your illness, as it is better able than we are to hand the illness over to the spirit world or to Mother Earth. In giving permission to plant spirits to carry out their work, we create the space for divine union and mutual reciprocity.

It is essential to let go of preconceived notions about how we think plants will assist us in our healing and what the outcome will be. We might need assistance with a form of cancer, but the plant spirit may instruct the healing energies of the plant to focus on anger issues that stem from childhood. Overall, trusting in Divine Providence creates a healthy, healing relationship between you and the plant, and letting go of your wounding—with great compassion—assists the process even further.

The following is an anonymous prayer that I use to remind myself of the journey we take with the plant spirits and the medicine we receive.

> *When the wind blows, that is my medicine.*
> *When it rains, that is my medicine.*
> *When it hails, that is my medicine.*
> *When it becomes clear after a storm,*
> *That is my medicine.*

The Power of Prayer in Healing

Life is a prayer. Every aspect of creation is, in essence, a prayer when we enter into conscious relationship with it. In working with plants, we enter into prayer the moment we acknowledge the divine attributes and healing qualities of a plant. Our relationship to the plant becomes the vehicle for our evolution as spiritual beings.

The action of grounding this prayer manifests in the healing work we do with the plants. Intention is vital, as it sets up the space for the energy to unfold and work in accordance with Divine Providence. An energetic matrix, through which the spiritual energies come, is formed by the ways in which we observe, see, touch, taste, and smell the living things around us. Respect for the plant and its spirit is very important, for they are the doorkeepers that lead to the higher dimensions. They are the ones who bring our prayers to the Highest Will.

In praying with the plant, we are saying, "I am in need of your assistance. I am ready to receive whatever is necessary for my healing and growth. I surrender my intentions in the light of the highest good, and will do my part in helping myself heal."

When we offer prayers, we are saying that we have faith in the miraculous healing abilities of the plant and its spirit. We are saying that we believe! In offering prayer at the beginning of our work, we align ourselves with the higher vibrational healing energies that come from Spirit. We invite Spirit to come into our lives and heal us. The exchange with the plant world is sacred and unique to each individual. We are not welcoming a new friend into our lives; we are welcoming ourselves back home.

Gratitude is the greatest prayer we can offer to Spirit and to the earth. Always remember that we are never alone, and we have many assistants and guides in every aspect of our lives. It is humbling to wake up and be grateful for life, and for the beauty of creation that surrounds us. In expressing gratitude, we are acknowledging the greater workings in our lives that carry us along the way. Having gratitude also fosters a sense of compassion and humility for life's mysteries, the world, and all of the world's peoples.

In the plant chapters in the second half of this book, the sections titled "The Spiritual and Emotional Properties" offer specific suggestions on when, how, and why to pray to a plant spirit. When I was working with these plants, I felt a prayer was given to me to access

You open your hand and satisfy the desire of every living thing.
—Psalm 145

higher states of consciousness to effect healing. Each prayer reflects the vibration of a specific spirit and the energies of spiritual, emotional, and physical healing. These powerful prayers are doorways to the Divine, and hold the space for the light to come through.

Making Plant Spirit Essences

Early in the process of conceiving this book, while I was working with plants and their spirits, it became clear to me that I should also include physical remedies designed to heal various ailments energetically, in addition to the more spiritual information about plants. I should use different plant parts in various ways, and should make plant essences, or remedies, from nature. Please keep in mind, however, that the remedies offered in the following pages are not cures. They work energetically to heal issues in spiritual, emotional, and physical states of being. Within each plant chapter, the section entitled "The Physical Healing Properties" lists physical ailments and how to use essences and various plant parts to address them. These remedies contain the vibrational healing energy of the relevant plant spirit.

With these teachings, my intention is to assist you in creating a healing relationship between yourself and the earth, and offer guidance for making your own medicines from nature. When you put a substance of your own creation and energy into your body, you nurture yourself with your own divine essence.

How to Make Your Own Plant Spirit Essence

In making an essence for your personal use, the most important tools are prayer, love, gratitude, and of course your relationship with the plant spirit as you journey with it. If you choose to make an essence to take internally, trust the plant spirit to tell you the most fertile time for harvesting the necessary plant parts. In the upcoming chart, I have listed the parts to be used for the plants included in this book.

You will need spring water, alcohol (such as vodka or brandy) as a preserving agent, the part of the plant used for the medicine, a clear glass bowl, a tincture bottle to put your remedy in, and your intuition. Follow you intuition; you will be guided as to the best time of day to harness the healing energies of the plant spirit. I suggest that you create a sacred space, and begin your journey with the plant spirit there. You might want to make your essence in the sun, in the night with the energy of the moon, or in a special meditation room.

Take the part of the plant you will be using and immerse it in a small, clear bowl filled with spring water. Intuit the amount of time needed for the healing energy of the plant and spirit to imbue the water. When the energies of both have aligned with the water and have been blessed by the Divine, your water is potentized and becomes a plant spirit essence. Place your essence in a secure, clean, one-ounce bottle in a proportion of four parts essence to one part alcohol, and your process is complete. The alcohol secures the earth element, while the plant spirit essence holds the space for the etheric. Much love, prayer, and vibrational plant spirit energy helps to create these medicines of the earth and sky.

Plant spirit essences usually have no adverse side effects. However, as with any medicinal, use them with caution and seek the advice of a medical professional when in doubt. Also keep in mind that since, like all plant medicines, they allow for the natural healing process of the self to unfold, suppressed physical symptoms might appear when you use them. Likewise, symptoms might become exacerbated, as in a healing crisis, before healing occurs. Unfamiliar and unexpressed emotions and all forms of toxicity may also surface as the body and its various levels become healed.

There are many instances, in the upcoming pages, where I suggest using an herbal massage oil. There are two ways to accomplish this:

1. Macerate (mash) about 2 ounces of dried herbs, or twice that amount of fresh herbs, with a mortar and pestle. Place the herbs in a 1 pint lidded jar and fill with the recommended oil. Let the mixture stand in a warm place for three days. Strain and bottle the oil, and it is ready to use.

2. Combine the herbs and oil in a pot that is large enough to hold both. Heat the mixture gently for 1 hour, keeping it uncovered. The temperature should remain under 200° F. Strain and bottle the mixture when cooled.

To make an infusion or tea:

Bring 1 pint of water to a full boil in a medium-size pot, then remove from the burner. Use 2 teaspoons of dry herb or 2 tablespoons of fresh herb, and place the herb in the heated water and cover the pot tightly. Allow it to steep for at least 20 minutes, depending on how strong you want it.

The plant parts in the following chart were used to make the remedies in this book. I ask you to follow your own intuition, as well as guidance you receive from the plant spirits. Use whichever plant parts you are drawn to using—consciousness changes every moment, as do the physical, emotional, and spiritual realms of our being and the collective universe. The vibrations of the plants and their parts mirror this.

Angelica	leaf		Motherwort	leaf
Astragalus	leaf		Mugwort	leaf
Black Cohosh	leaf		Mullein	leaf
Blessed Thistle	leaf		Nettles	leaf
Calendula	leaf		Pulsatilla	leaf, flower, stem
Chamomile	leaf & flower		Poke	plant spirit only
Clematis	leaf		Red Clover	leaf
Dandelion	leaf & flower		Rosemary	leaf
Feverfew	leaf		Rue	leaf
Lamb's Ear	leaf		Sage	leaf
Lavender	leaf		Skullcap	leaf
Lemon Balm	leaf		St. John's Wort	leaf
Licorice	leaf		Violet	leaf
Lilac	leaf & flower		Wormwood	leaf
Marshmallow	leaf		Yarrow	leaf

THE PLANTS

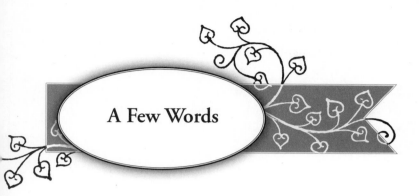

A Few Words

This part of the book focuses specifically on the spiritual, emotional, and physical healing properties of thirty plants. I received the information through various intuitive means. What manifested out of my apprenticeship in this work are novel and ancient teachings about working with plant medicines. In this section are those plants whose words most need to be heard.

As I journeyed with the plants, their spirits came to me and shared their stories. I sat in meditation with each plant as its spirit told me what the plant can address spiritually, emotionally, and physically. Some of this information was communicated through clairaudience; other information was passed to me kinesthetically, as the vibration of the physical illness passed through my body. With each plant came a prayer—an invocation and gesture of gratitude for the work and knowledge that was shared.

I found that the vibration and peak healing frequency varied from plant to plant. In some of the following remedies, you will see time frames given as to when it is best to utilize the remedy. In Oriental medicine, each organ of the human body corresponds with a time of day at which the energy of the organ is at its strongest or weakest; the time frames I've included are given for a reason. When I communicated with the plant spirits, I would work near a plant and ask its permission to harvest and hold the parts that were to be used for healing purposes. At the end of the communication, I noticed that the parts that I held were withered, and that the life force of the plant had passed through my body, showing me its energies and the illness it healed. Their nectar became aligned with my life force, as it is with all living things.

After giving its life and healing, the plant spirit would leave, and the plant part would literally die. I was moved by this, and I wondered how we could honor the earth and harvest the medicines sparingly, so as to avoid unnecessary destruction of plant life. Upon completing my work with each plant, I again offered my gratitude and devotion.

Yet despite the physical death of plant parts, plant spirits remain alive and vibrant! It is the plant spirit who nurtures new growth to come. Each plant part has served its purpose as part of Divine Providence, and the plant will regenerate with the help of its spirit. After experiencing the unconditionally loving generosity of each plant that I worked with, I would place the withered part next to the plant from which it came, so that Mother Earth could cradle it gently in her arms.

With the earth today in such a state of change and unrest, and with many species of plants being overharvested and dying out, we need to search for new ways of utilizing our most precious resources, and earth's creations, with care and gentleness. The evolution of time and consciousness is rapidly changing. The earth itself, and its people and their illnesses, are also changing in matter, vibration, and essence. The way we use medicines has to change if we are ever to heal ourselves and the earth and preserve our resources. If we can begin to use medicines vibrationally, it will do much to preserve our resources and effect healing in a more precise way.

When you work vibrationally with plant medicine, you use the plants in conjunction with the vibration of what you are trying to heal, whatever its level. In this way, you utilize less of the plant and more of its spirit. In doing this, you will also begin to utilize plant medicines differently. Preparation methods and best times to use the medicine will be communicated to you by the plant spirits. Remember, less is more. I have often seen that a few drops of an earth medicine taken in accordance with a body's needs can have more of an effect than a plant-derived medicine taken at full dosage.

In working with the earth in this new but ancient way, you will learn to truly respect the plants, their medicine, and their healing powers. You will also give yourself and the land time to produce healthier gardens, and you will create medicines that will benefit all of humankind.

Angelica
Plant Spirit Prayer

....

Sages of Old, bestow unto us your blessings of guidance and protection.

....

Angelica
(Angelica archangelica)

My Experience with This Plant Spirit

When I call on the spirit of angelica, not one but many elementals come to assist. They look like children, young girls and boys, but are old souls who have lived in the spirit world for centuries. They possess gifts of magic and wizardry and their role is to protect all men, women, and children from harm. Since they cannot leave their dimension, they harvest many angelica plants on earth to do their work for them. Through ritual, they imbue the plants with special powers to protect and heal us.

The Spiritual and Emotional Properties

Angelica is a protective plant. It secures one's boundaries, and protects against negative influences, spells, and curses. It assists those who cannot stand up for themselves and who are prone to vulnerability. It acts as a filter for those who communicate with the spirit world, and protects the psychic field.

Angelica represents the duality of life, the light and dark sides of nature that need to coexist in a harmonious state. Call on the spirit of angelica if you are having a nervous breakdown. It helps to alleviate severe emotional stress and loss of emotional control, naturally numbing the emotional nervous system when it is overwhelmed. Angelica is excellent in reducing hypersensitivity in people, especially in those who are energetically sensitive.

The Physical Healing Properties

Do not use when pregnant.

Angelica is excellent for healing the pain of headaches. Upon the onset of the pain, take 3 drops of the essence in water and sip slowly.

It also helps to alleviate high blood pressure. Place a drop of the essence under your tongue when needed, or massage a mixture of drops of the essence with almond oil onto your chest.

Angelica is also very good at healing the energy around angina and heart attacks. Make a compress of fresh leaves and place on the chest area for 20-minute intervals. Do this by moistening the leaves with a little warmed water and placing them between folded layers of cotton cloth.

For fevers, use the same compress and place it on the forehead until the fever is reduced.

For colicky babies, make a massage oil of the leaves and flowers in olive oil, and massage a small amount onto the baby's back.

Angelica acts as a natural stimulant and antibiotic when used homeopathically in sick children. When the need arises, place a few drops of the essence in water for the child to sip slowly. Do not use this with children under the age of five.

Angelica promotes the onset of the menstrual cycle. Take 2 drops of the essence in water daily until one begins to menstruate.

It energetically tonifies the prostate in men and strengthens the uterus in women. Place angelica plants around you or take a drop of the essence under your tongue upon retiring. Only do this when you need tonification one of those areas.

Angelica also helps in extreme cases of mental handicap and nervous breakdown by calming the nervous system. Place the plants around you or take a drop of the essence in water and sip slowly.

ASTRAGALUS
PLANT SPIRIT PRAYER

....

Gracious One, we are honored by your presence. We seek the knowledge of the mysteries of our existence. We seek to know ourselves, as we are lost from our essence. Bring us home.

....

Astragalus
(*Astragalus membranaceus*)

My Experience with This Plant Spirit

When I call upon the spirit of the plant, an elderly Asian man appears to me. He is a medicine man and a magician, very mysterious in his ways and mannerisms. He doesn't say much, yet has the ability to heal the broken aspects of one's soul without uttering a word. He sits in his little and very simplistic kitchen, always cooking something over the fire for those who come to visit him. And many do. They come from everywhere and are not even sure why; but somehow they become drawn to this mysterious man.

As I envision him, he shows me he is with a stranger who has wandered in, looking lost and confused. The elderly man sits at his kettle stirring a mixture of hot water and herbs, one of which is astragalus. Also, gracefully moving in the kettle are special worms taken from his garden. These worms are gifted with medicinal and spiritual healing qualities, and continue to thrive as the kettle simmers. They form a symbol around each astragalus leaf—the yin/yang symbol—and imbue the plant with masculine and feminine healing energies. When the medicine is finished cooking, the worms are put back in the garden to rejuvenate themselves for future healings.

The elderly man offers the stranger a cup of the medicine, knowing that its power will help to bring back the stranger's soul, which was lost long ago. The man drinks from the cup and travels on his way, not aware of the powers that will now work in his life. The elderly man sends the stranger off with a nod and returns to his simplicity. As the stranger heads down the road, if you stare closely enough, you might see a myriad of sparks floating around him as he walks, and a glow in his eyes that has been missing for a while...his soul has returned!

The Spiritual and Emotional Properties

Call on the spirit of astragalus when you are feeling a sense of soul loss. This plant is very gifted in searching out lost souls.

Also use astragalus when you are feeling emotionally shut down in general and cannot let anyone in...the plant will help you to open up. This plant spirit will always be there for you, to follow you into those deep and dark places of your life.

When your spirit leaves your body, astragalus will find it and bring it back to where it belongs. Call on the spirit of astragalus when you are on a journey discovering or rediscovering yourself.

Astragalus is excellent for helping with boundaries. It is also excellent for fostering respect for yourself and others.

The vibration of the plant is at the doorway of the lower world of physical reality, thus helping to watch over it. It is also comforting to spirits, and is very useful in long-distance healing work when working at the level of the soul.

The Physical Healing Properties

Do not use when pregnant.

Astragalus helps to heal the energy surrounding convulsions and head injuries. Make a compress of dried leaves by moistening the leaves with a little warmed water and placing them between folded layers of cotton cloth. Place the compress over the injury for 30-minute intervals.

To balance the electrolytes in the body, as well as nourish the body when it is vitamin deficient, take 1–2 drops of astragalus essence in water.

Astragalus nourishes the energy of the heart. Take 1–3 drops of the essence in water between one and three o'clock in the afternoon.

Astragalus is also a good remedy for balancing the nervous system; take 1 drop under the tongue upon waking. And it can help when one is unable to sleep due to anxiety or nervous energy; take 1 drop of the essence in water before going to bed.

For cleansing the gall bladder and alleviating the pain of gallstones, make a compress of fresh or dried astragalus moistened with water, placing the herb between folded layers of cotton cloth. Place this over the gall bladder. Massage the area first with warmed castor oil, and place a heating pad on top of the compress. Do this for 20-minute intervals.

Using a salve of astragalus is excellent for healing cuts and bruises; it also helps to heal the energy around throat operations, past or present. Make a massage oil from the herb and olive oil, and massage the warmed oil onto the throat area.

Taking a few drops of the essence under the tongue upon waking will help to balance your hormones. Calling on the plant spirit while bathing with the leaves is a good remedy that will balance your masculine and feminine energies.

BLACK COHOSH
PLANT SPIRIT PRAYER

....

*O sacred grounds of the earth, lull our spirits to rest upon your divine
heartbeat. Take from us our pain so that
you may transform it with your profound healing energy.*

....

Black Cohosh
(Cimicifuga racemosa)

My Experience with This Plant Spirit

When I call on the spirit of black cohosh, a ceremonial dance of tribal Native American women comes into my vision. There is one among them who is a medicine woman, a healer, and a peacemaker. She leads the others in a ritual dance of prayer and offering to Mother Earth and the spirits who help her. As the medicine woman chants a prayer to the earth, she moves her body upward toward the sky and then reaches downward, allowing her entire being to touch and merge with the ground. In this dance, she offers herself and the soul of her womb to the Mother, cradling the earth as she does to find comfort and peace. As she merges, she takes branches of the black cohosh plant in her hands to give as an offering. Upon touching the earth, the branches become imbued with the sacred healing properties of the energies of the Mother.

The Spiritual and Emotional Properties

Call on the spirit of black cohosh to protect yourself from evil spirits and spirit possession. It is used in sacred ceremony to draw out spirits and ancestors from the body. It is also used as an offering to Mother Earth, because of the special relationship it holds to that energy. Black cohosh nourishes and honors the Mother. It is a plant that shows reverence to the wise and ancient ways of the ancestors.

Call on the spirit of black cohosh to assist you if you have to give up a child for adoption. It will help to protect and also heal the energy surrounding the child. It is a healing force for parents when a child is lost to trauma, physically, mentally, emotionally, or spiritually, and is excellent for healing the spiritual and emotional challenges around infertility.

Black cohosh can also be called on for the protection of the community. It guards against damaging fires, droughts, floods, and the threat of imminent danger. It will also protect little children and animals from harm.

Call on the spirit of black cohosh to care for those who are entering into an uncomfortable and challenging situation. It is used to create and hold sacred space in ceremony and ritual. It is also used as an offering and gift to the spirits for doing their work.

The Physical Healing Properties

Do not use when pregnant. It can induce miscarriage and abortion.

Black cohosh is excellent for healing the energy around hysteria and mental illness. Call on the spirit of the plant to assist you, and place many plants near you when you sleep. Adding 5–10 drops of the plant spirit essence in water a few times a day will also help.

For uterine cramping, take 4 drops of the essence under your tongue at the onset of the discomfort. Also make an oil using the leaves of black cohosh and almond oil, and massage it onto the pelvic area.

For nosebleeds, massage a mixture of a few drops of the essence and warmed olive oil onto your nose after the bleeding stops. It will help heal the energy in the tissue.

For excessive menstrual bleeding, take 3–5 drops of the essence in water upon retiring, and also massage a mixture of drops of the essence with St. John's wort oil onto the pelvic area. For extreme pain in the uterus, burn the dry leaves of black cohosh around you, and also make a poultice to place on the pelvic area (place fresh leaves on your pelvic area). Massage the area first with warmed olive oil. Do the same for healing the energies around fibroids, cysts, and tumors.

To heal the energy around breast cancer, take 5 drops of the essence in water upon waking. Also place many plants around you as you sleep, and massage a mixture of a few drops of the essence and almond oil onto the breast area.

For healing the energy around cervical cancer, place a compress of the leaves, moistened with a little warmed water, on top of the pubic bone. Place the moistened leaves between layers of folded cotton cloth and leave it on for 20-minute intervals. Do not exceed more than twice a day.

For bladder dysfunction in men, make an oil of the leaves and almond oil and massage the warmed oil onto the bladder area. This is best done upon retiring. It is also beneficial to place a white cloth over the bladder area while you sleep. For men who suffer from a hernia, massage drops of the essence with warmed almond oil onto the area.

Black cohosh is excellent for heart stress and pain in the chest. Make a compress of the fresh leaves by putting the leaves, moistened with water, between folded layers of cotton cloth, and place atop the chest area for 10-minute intervals. For relaxing the body, reducing stress, and calming the nervous system, place a drop of the essence under your tongue.

BLESSED THISTLE
PLANT SPIRIT PRAYER

....

Tender heart, take hold of those who yearn for companionship and nurturing. Bring to them a love of purity, kindness, and gentleness that will be with them the rest of their days.

....

Blessed Thistle
(Cnicus benedictus)

My Experience with This Plant Spirit

When I call on the spirit of blessed thistle, a wise old man appears to me. He walks with a limp and uses a cane to help him in his travels. When he is not walking, he spends much of his time in a rocker he carved out of wood. He is a quiet spirit, rocking back and forth in his chair and watching the lives of many of us here. He tends to be a little grumpy at times, but don't let that fool you. Behind that is a spirit with a heart of gold. He is a caretaker of all the people who are left alone in this world, especially the elderly. Surrounding him are many blessed thistle plants. They seem to have an overabundance of heart energy to give to others. Every time the wise man sees a person whose heart is worn from feeling alone, he blesses a blessed thistle, and with its permission extracts heart energy and sends it to the person in need of healing.

The Spiritual and Emotional Properties

Call on the spirit of blessed thistle to guide you in your prayers. It fosters self-forgiveness and brings with it compassion and absolution for past grievances and mistakes. It is useful in helping locate something you have lost. It soothes irritability and frustration, and can assist you in concentrating on yourself and your life's work. It is used in celebrations, gatherings, and ceremonies as a gifting to whatever is being honored. Blessed thistle helps to bring peace to those recovering from long-term illness, balances the heart energy in relationships, and is excellent in calming cranky babies and children.

Call on the spirit of blessed thistle to help those who are codependent and tend to take on other people's issues. It will create boundaries around the heart and bring the person's focus back inward. Blessed thistle is an energetic protector of the skeleto-muscular system of the human body; call on it to keep company with elderly people who are in need of attention and care. For older people who tend to injure themselves all the time, place blessed thistle plants around them to work with the emotional energies of such injuries.

The Physical Healing Properties

Do not use when pregnant.

Blessed thistle is excellent for detoxifying the liver and gall bladder. Create a compress of the leaves by taking fresh or dried leaves and placing them in a generous amount of warmed castor oil. Steep the leaves for at least a half-hour in the oil, then place them between layers of folded cotton cloth. Place the compress on the liver and gall bladder area for 20–30 minutes. This is best done before retiring.

Blessed thistle is a good remedy for strengthening eyesight. Take a drop of the plant spirit essence under your tongue upon waking. Also place a compress of the dry leaves, moistened with a touch of warm water and placed between layers of folded cotton cloth, over the closed eyes. Leave on the eyes for 5 minutes.

If you find that your immune system is weakened, place 10 drops of the essence of blessed thistle in water once daily. Blessed thistle clears brain fog and improves the functioning of the brain; take 3 drops of the essence in water upon waking. It also detoxifies the entire body system—bathe with the fresh leaves of blessed thistle in order to provide nutrients and vitamins to the blood. You can also place a few drops of the essence in warm water and drink as a tea upon waking.

Blessed thistle assists in regulating the energy of the thymus gland. Massage a mixture of drops of the essence, St. John's wort oil, and almond oil onto the area of the thymus. It also assists in regulating the energetics of blood pressure.

Massage a mixture of a few drops of the essence mixed with warmed apricot oil onto the chest and heart area. This will improve circulation and assists in bringing oxygen to the cells. Make an oil of the leaves of blessed thistle and almond oil and massage over the body after bathing.

Blessed thistle can assist in relieving menstrual cramping and bloating, and in regulating the energies of female hormones. Make an oil from the leaves of blessed thistle, the leaves of lavender, and almond oil, and massage onto the pelvic area.

It is also helpful in the healing of pain associated with arthritis. Make a mixture of drops of the essence, a few drops of rose geranium essential oil, and almond oil; massage it onto affected areas after bathing.

Blessed thistle detoxifies the bladder and kidneys. Make an oil from fresh or dried leaves and wheat germ oil, and massage the warmed oil onto the kidney and bladder areas after bathing.

Last but not least, blessed thistle assists in healing and balancing the heart energy. Place blessed thistle plants around you, or take a drop of the essence under your tongue.

CALENDULA
PLANT SPIRIT PRAYER

....

*Play with me, O joyful one, and shine your radiance
under the sun. Bring comfort, joy and innocence to all,
for we behold your beauty in one so small.*

....

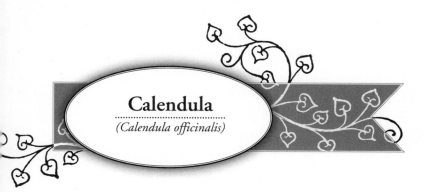

Calendula
(Calendula officinalis)

My Experience with This Plant Spirit

When I call on the spirit of calendula, I see a vision of an adorable little girl. She is surrounded by butterflies and kneeling in an enchanted garden of God's creation. She communicates with all of God's creatures, as many are drawn to her innocence. She is completely joyous and filled with the beauty that surrounds her. The sun shines and radiates its warmth through her very core. Flowering next to her is a vibrant calendula flower. Its petals are open toward the gentleness of the little spirit's face, as if to take in her very essence. She becomes smitten at once with the softness and radiance of its colors and leaves, and pulls the bloom in close to her to dance upon its magic. The moment she touches it, she also shares with the plant her innocence and jubilation and the two become friends for eternity, helping others to heal.

The Spiritual and Emotional Properties

The spirit of calendula helps children in many ways. Call on it to help them laugh, play, and get along better, or to comfort children who might feel alone. Calendula brings comfort to children whose parents are separated or divorced, as well as to children when one parent is not living at home anymore. It helps children who are having difficulty with relationships with other kids. Also call on the spirit of the plant to help bring life back to children whose souls seem to have left them at a very early age due to some form of abandonment and neglect; calendula will comfort them and bring them playful spiritual energies to fill their days. Calendula also fosters a sense of appropriate sexual energetic boundaries for children who might not have them.

Likewise, calendula brings playful, childlike energy to all who touch it. It can heal the inner child on a deep level, bringing jubilation and joy to your life. It carries a sense of innocence and can help you create that in your life. It nurtures an adult's sensual and sexual energy and can help you feel more attractive. It helps attract your soul mate.

The Physical Healing Properties

Calendula is excellent for tonifying the thymus gland. Make an oil from the leaves of calendula and almond oil, and massage the warmed oil over the area of the thymus. Also, placing a drop of the plant spirit essence in water upon waking is helpful.

Calendula increases sexual energy and libido. Place many plants around yourself and your partner before you retire. Also take 4 drops of the essence in water and sip slowly upon retiring.

To improve brain function, take a drop of the essence in water when needed. To strengthen heart energy, make a compress of calendula leaves by moistening the leaves with water and placing them between layers of folded cotton cloth. Place this on top of the chest for 15 minutes. This is best done in the early evening.

Calendula is useful for drawing toxins out of the kidneys. Make an oil with fresh leaves and flowers and wheat germ oil, and massage this warmed oil onto the kidneys after bathing.

To alleviate muscle tension, make a mixture of drops of the essence and olive oil, and massage it onto muscles after bathing.

Calendula also energetically repels parasites within the digestive tract. Place the leaves onto your stomach for 20-minute intervals. The parasites will be energetically drawn to the leaves and will assist the departure on the physical level.

To stimulate a sluggish gall bladder, make an oil from the leaves of a rosemary plant and almond oil. Mix a few drops of calendula essence into this oil and massage it onto the gall bladder area.

To heal the energy around abnormal cell growth in the uterus and cervix, make a compress by moistening calendula flowers and leaves with warmed almond oil and placing them between layers of folded cotton cloth. Massage the uterine and cervix area with warmed St. John's wort oil, then place the compress onto the pubic area for 30-minute intervals.

Calendula is excellent for knee, hip, and other joint injuries. Make an oil of the leaves and flowers and olive oil, then massage it onto affected areas after bathing. Do the same for nerve pain in the legs.

Chamomile
Plant Spirit Prayer

....

In the angelic whisper of light and love,
may we fall upon your wings to shelter us from harm
and give us everlasting hope.

....

Chamomile
(Matricaria recutita)

My Experience with This Plant Spirit

When I call upon the spirit of chamomile, a beautiful butterfly comes whispering through the air. Her soft wings flutter aimlessly as she carries herself gently and with ease. The joy of freedom and nonattachment is the gift she bears, and she travels with this from the luminescent clouds to the earth. She is drawn to the chamomile flower, and lands on its tiny petals. Being a messenger, she stays for just a short while, then carries herself back to the clouds where an angel awaits her return. With open arms and wings of silver, the angel embraces the butterfly and imbues her with angelic healing qualities to bring back to the chamomile plant. Enhanced by the angel's touch, the butterfly departs, magic gracing her wings. She dances from one chamomile flower to another, bringing the many blessings of the angels above.

The Spiritual and Emotional Properties

Call on the spirit of chamomile when there is confusion. It helps to bring about a sense of calmness, and creates space in which you can sort things out. It fosters a sense of self-dignity and pride and works to balance emotions and thought patterns, especially the energy and emotion of unexpressed or over-expressed rage.

Chamomile is very helpful when you are depressed. It is excellent for healing the emotional energies around addiction, specifically the emotional energies around alcoholism. It is useful when one is cognizant of dying, and helps to foster a sense of inner peace. It brings calmness when imminent threat or danger is near.

The Physical Healing Properties

Chamomile works to shift the energy around convulsions. Place 10 drops of the essence under the tongue at the onset of the condition.

It helps to alleviate headaches. Take 5–10 drops of the essence in water at the onset of pain.

Chamomile helps calm diarrhea; take 3 drops three times a day in water until the condition subsides. It also helps calm nausea, vomiting, and tummy ache; make an infusion of the flowers, or place drops of the essence in warm water.

If you have a virus or influenza, chamomile can help strengthen the energetic body. Drink the tea made of fresh or dried flowers, or place 2 drops of the essence under the tongue upon waking each morning until you begin to feel better.

Since chamomile bring nutrients to the bone and maintains bone density in men and women as they age, consider taking a few drops of the essence in water daily, or drinking a tea made of the flowers, to aid this process.

To soothe diaper rash, make an infusion of the fresh flowers in almond oil, and massage it onto your baby's skin.

Chamomile also helps heal rashes from poison ivy and poison oak. Make an oil from the fresh flowers, St. John's wort flowers or essence, and almond oil, and massage it lightly onto the affected areas.

Chamomile is a great muscle relaxer. Place a few drops under your tongue when your muscles are feeling a bit stressed!

For tooth pain, make an infusion of fresh flowers or essence with olive oil, and massage it onto your gums.

Clematis
Plant Spirit Prayer

....

*We gather here today as your children, the children of the
Beloved One Spirit that unites us all. We ask that we be strengthened
in your holy love and be guided to teach the ways of goodness to
all peoples of the earth.*

....

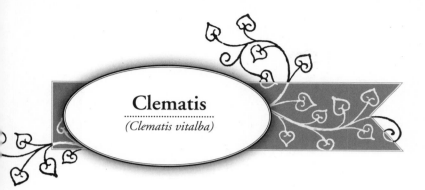

Clematis
(Clematis vitalba)

My Experience with This Plant Spirit

When I call on the spirit of clematis, a vibrant and colorful woman comes into my vision. She is of indigenous heritage and projects great strength and wisdom. A gatherer of people of all ages and cultures, she regally summons those who are called to listen to her message. Many come and sit by her and listen to her words.

She shares with us that we all need to take care of each other. No matter who we are or what we look like, we have to respect each other's differences. She says that we must look beyond appearances, deep within our hearts. We are all the same, of one God. Then she gathers the people in closer and asks everyone to join hands. She holds up a clematis, representing all who have gathered to honor universal love and consciousness. She looks around intently and reminds everyone to love each other as we want to be loved. After making a blessing over the plant, she asks everyone to silently say their own blessings and send that energy to the clematis. It is this powerful union that imbues clematis with its awesome healing abilities.

The Spiritual and Emotional Properties

Call on the spirit of clematis for strength in expressing yourself; clematis gives those who cannot speak a voice. It brings healing for self-judgment, self-loathing, and jealousy.

Clematis likewise brings healing to those who are selfish and self-absorbed, not giving to others or humanity. It heals dishonesty by fostering a conscious awakening in people. For those who push their way through life without regard for others, clematis nudges them to look beyond themselves.

Call on clematis to heal those who are ruthless in their actions. It is the plant of universal love and conscious awakening, fostering a sense of selflessness in people and creating an environment of sharing. It encourages community and reciprocity. It improves humanity's ability to give to one another out of love, and helps to heal hunger, cultural differences, and domestic violence.

The Physical Healing Properties

Clematis helps to heal the energy around genital herpes. Take 4–5 drops of the essence in water upon awakening. You can also place clematis plants next to you while you sleep, or soak in a bath imbued with clematis flowers. Clematis also helps heal the herpes-related virus that causes mouth ulcers or canker sores; take a few drops of the essence under your tongue upon waking.

Clematis is useful in the healing of intestinal yeast and fungus; place a drop daily under your tongue upon waking. For skin rashes associated with viral infections, make an infusion of the leaves and almond oil and mildly massage it onto the skin. (Do not use if there are open sores.)

For constipation, massage a mixture of warmed wheat germ oil and drops of clematis essence onto the pelvis and lower back.

For worms in the digestive tract, make an infusion of warmed wheat germ oil and clematis leaves and massage it onto the digestive areas.

Clematis assists in healing the energies surrounding epileptic seizures, dementia, and spasmodic fits. Place many plants around you and call on the spirit for assistance.

Clematis also has a purifying effect on the blood. Place a drop of the essence in water and take as needed.

For heavy loss of blood due to miscarriages, place a few drops of the essence in a mixture of almond oil and St. John's wort oil, and massage it onto the pelvis.

DANDELION
PLANT SPIRIT PRAYER

....

Joyful Spirit, full of glee, fill me, embrace me, and shelter me.
Make this magic of the most high,
grant my dreams unto the sky.

....

Dandelion
(Taraxacum officinale)

My Experience with This Plant Spirit

In calling on the spirit of dandelion, I discovered that my eyes had to be quick to catch this whimsical and magical young lad! But it's not hard to find him; if you look at a beautiful rainbow in the sky, you will see him sitting there with his eyes open wide and a smile as big as the rainbow itself. He is a jovial young boy—who wouldn't be jovial sitting atop a pot of gold coins amidst those brilliant colors? Lost from his family at birth, he receives joy and healing through creating magic and granting people's wishes. When I invoke the spirit of dandelion, this young lad takes one of the gold coins from the pot, brings it to his mouth, and blows into it. In the wink of an eye, he is surrounded by sparkling fireflies. He then turns the gold coin into a magnificent dandelion flower, and gives it to all those hoping to make their wishes come true.

The Spiritual and Emotional Properties

Call on the spirit of dandelion when you are faced with depression and inconsolable grief. It assists when you are feeling hopeless, having lost your way in the world. It also helps you to be in relationship with the yearning and longing that comes from keeping your integrity as you navigate life's challenges. It gives you strength as you step into the dark night of the soul, searching for the light at the end of the tunnel.

Dandelion can help heal the relationship between a mother and daughter, and assists in repairing the family structure. This plant spirit is also excellent in working with sudden trauma, loss, or shock; it immediately works to help bring understanding of a situation to your heart, and eases the integration and acceptance process. Also call on dandelion for abundance and good fortune!

The Physical Healing Properties

Dandelion is a good remedy for healing the energy surrounding hardened arteries. Make a poultice using 2 parts root and 1 part leaf, and place it on the sternum between the breasts. Do this for 20-minute intervals, no more than 3 times per day. Fresh or dried herb can be used.

To help heal sinus pressure and headache, make a mixture using 12 drops of dandelion essence per tablespoon of olive oil and massage it onto the sinus cavity, outward and down toward the neck. Also rub it along the top of the cervical spine, reaching toward the occipital ridge at the base of the cranium.

For mucus in the lungs, make a mixture of 20 drops of the essence in ¼ cup warmed wheat germ oil, and massage it into the chest.

For low blood pressure, rub a few drops of the essence mixed with almond oil onto the wrist pulse points, and also on the inside of the foot.

For poor circulation, mix the essence with almond oil and self-massage daily after bathing.

For cervical dysplasia (abnormal cell growth in the cervix), make a compress of dried dandelion leaves moistened with warm water in a ratio of 2:1. Take the moistened leaves and place them between layers of folded cotton cloth. Place the compress atop the pubic bone, which has first been massaged with warm castor oil, for 20-minute intervals. Late morning to early afternoon is the best time for this.

For fluid retention from diabetes, make a compress of fresh flowers and warm olive oil, taking the moistened flowers and placing them between layers of folded cotton cloth. Place the compress on the top of the head for 15 minutes. If fresh flowers are not available for your compress, use 2 tablespoons of warmed castor oil and add 10 drops of the essence; place this compress on the forehead for 10-minute intervals.

FEVERFEW
PLANT SPIRIT PRAYER

···

*Wanderer of the inner plane, help us to seek that which we yearn to find
so deeply within ourselves.
Guide us in bringing forth that essence to
nurture those we love with it.*

···

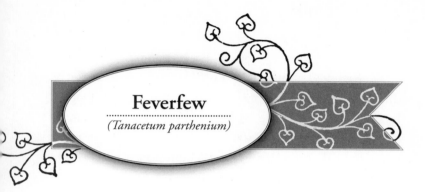

Feverfew
(Tanacetum parthenium)

My Experience with This Plant Spirit

When I call on the spirit of feverfew, a weeping male apparition arrives. He carries with him so much sorrow for the
life he left behind on earth. He crossed over into the spirit
world very suddenly, and has many regrets about not spend-
ing enough time with those he loved or getting to know
himself more deeply. His face is withered from emotion; his
cloak of pale green is worn from traveling the inner planes
in search of one more chance.

In his quest to honor himself, he has made a promise to
help heal and protect relationships. He travels the ethers to
every corner of the world, watching over homes and families
and sending healing energies to them. Whenever a family
becomes blessed with his healing, a feverfew plant will grow
in close proximity to them. If you stumble across feverfew or
use it for medicinal purposes, know that it is imbued with
the healing energies of relationship.

The Spiritual and Emotional Properties

Feverfew carries a lot of light. Call on its spirit to ward off negative energies and spirits. Place it at your door when loved ones are coming home after a long time away; feverfew holds the sacred space when conflict and healing need to happen. It brings longevity to age, and helps those who are constantly busy create time for their families. It helps people to get in touch with their creativity and the feminine aspects of the self. It brings artistry to your view of reality.

Feverfew heals the energy of male insecurity and the energy of long-held grief and regret. It can assist you in making compromises and helps you to enjoy life. It works to balance pride, keep honor and integrity at your place of work, and heal the energy around financial burdens. Call on the spirit of feverfew to protect you in the ocean.

The Physical Healing Properties

Feverfew is excellent for healing the energy around nerve pain. Take 5 drops of the essence in water upon waking.

For reducing fevers, make a compress of the leaves by moistening them with a little warmed water and placing them between layers of folded cotton cloth. Place the compress on the forehead for 20-minute intervals.

For headaches, place a few drops of feverfew essence in water and sip slowly at the onset of pain.

For chills, place feverfew plants around you.

For throat infections, tonsillitis, and strep throat, make a mixture from drops of the essence, warmed wheat germ oil, and St. John's wort oil. Massage this onto the throat area.

For ear infections, make a mixture from drops of the essence and warmed olive oil, and massage it around the ear and on the outer part of the inside of the ear.

For congestion in the lungs, make an infusion of the leaves and flowers with warmed almond oil and massage it onto the chest area.

To relieve nausea, place a drop of the essence under your tongue. For worms and other toxins in the stomach and digestive tract, take 10–15 drops of the essence in water daily as needed. Feverfew balances and tonifies the liver chi; place a few drops of the essence in warmed almond oil and massage it onto the liver area.

Just calling on the spirit of the plant and having feverfew around you will help heal the energies around learning disabilities, as well as the energy around impotence for men. It promotes the energy of fertility, and makes the womb and uterus more receptive to communion. Calling on feverfew and having it around you also protects women during pregnancy when complications arise. It assists with the energy flow of women having uterine contractions, and protects the mother as she is about to give birth.

LAMB'S EAR
PLANT SPIRIT PRAYER

....

Holy Father, Holy Mother, Most Powerful of all beings, we call on your divine assistance to hear our prayers. We ask in thy name to send forth the power of the Holy Spirit to make manifest the miraculous healing abilities of our enlightened ones. We ask this in accordance with the will of God.

....

Lamb's Ear
(Stachys byzantina)

My Experience with This Plant Spirit

When I call on the spirit of lamb's ear, an elderly male form appears out of the ethers. He is surrounded by penetrating rays of yellow light. White hair embraces the wrinkles on his tender face, which is partially covered by the beard he has grown for many years. He wears a modest cloak; he likes to travel lightly as he has much healing work to do. Every time lamb's ear makes a request for healing, he makes a journey to answer its prayers.

Near the sacred shrub, protecting it, is a beautiful lamb with large and sparkling eyes and a brilliant white coat. He guards the plant and all of the prayers that are made in honor of its name. Every morning, he places his tiny ear next to the leaves and listens to the many requests made for healing. When the time comes for the prayers to be answered, the elderly male spirit approaches the lamb and places one of his hands gently over its head, the other over the plant.

He imbues the animal and the plant with holy energy, thus activating lamb's ear's miraculous healing abilities.

The Spiritual and Emotional Properties

Call on the spirit of lamb's ear when you feel agitated and frustrated with life; it can help you come to terms with things more peacefully and with less conflict. It is a very special plant, teaching patience, acceptance, and surrender to what life brings to us. It shows us how to struggle less and allow our path to unfold.

Lamb's ear also helps us make peace with things that serve us no longer. It fosters self-love and forgiveness, and aids in the natural process of letting go. It is the plant of surrendering. It brings understanding and peace when one is challenged with major illness. It nourishes our creativity and intuition. It brings sexual innocence back to those who feel they have lost it due to trauma.

Lamb's ear comforts newborn babies. Place leaves of this plant around very sick children—it will bring them much protection and help in a speedy recovery. It also helps people overcome shyness. Call on this plant spirit to help you transition from puberty to adolescence to adulthood!

The Physical Healing Properties

Lamb's ear is excellent in energetically assisting in the healing process around heart attacks, arrhythmia, and strokes. Make a large compress by taking the leaves and moistening them with a little warmed water. Place the moistened leaves between folded layers of cotton cloth. Add a few sprigs of violet, and place the compress on the chest for 20-minute intervals. Do this as needed.

Lamb's ear is also helpful in healing the energies around epilepsy and seizure disorders. Make a large compress of fresh leaves from both lamb's ear and mullein; do this by moistening the leaves with water and placing them between layers of folded cotton cloth. Place the compress on the top of the head for an hour.

For poor eyesight, make a compress of fresh lamb's ear leaves moistened with warm water and place it over the eyes for 5–7 minutes. This is best done in the morning. For a low functioning thyroid, take a dosage of 2 drops of the essence in water per day. This is best done upon waking.

Lamb's ear also is used as a gentle tonifier of the overall endocrine system. Take a dosage of 3 drops under the tongue in the early morning. Do this as needed. It also tonifies the male reproductive system and prostate glands; take 2–6 drops of essence in water per day.

Lamb's ear is sacred in that it assists in healing the energies surrounding cancers—for example, prostate, esophagus, lung, intestinal, uterine, and cervical cancers. Take 10–20 drops of the essence in water per day. Remember that it is important to consult with your health care practitioner whenever utilizing any alternative methods in conjunction with treatments you are already using for your illness.

Lamb's ear is excellent in assisting in the recovery of rape and sexual violence victims, and healing the disconnection that might arise in the person's spirit. Take one drop under the tongue in the early morning, and massage a mixture of almond oil and drops of lamb's ear essence onto the pelvic area. See yourself surrounded by blue light and held safely by Spirit.

LAVENDER
PLANT SPIRIT PRAYER

....

O gentle angel with the light of spirit, come dance upon me.
Wrap your wings around my soul and send unto my heart
the light you hold.

....

Lavender
(Lavandula angustifolia)

My Experience with This Plant Spirit

When I call on the spirit of lavender, a vision of a summer garden appears to me. A beautiful young mother is sitting in the sun with her newborn infant cradled in her arms. She is nursing her child, feeding it fresh warm milk from her breasts as the sun shines upon the baby's face. Mother and child are nestled serenely among lavender plants, whose gentle fragrance fills the air around them. The mother laughs in utter joy and smiles as she looks down at her child. Having received the mother's nourishment, the child coos and grasps onto her nipple for security. The bond between them is strong and sacred.

Drawn to its hypnotic scent, the mother reaches over to take a sprig of lavender from the plant. She brings it close so that her child can smell it, and then places it in her hair. She watches as her child's face lights up and the two of them become bathed in an effervescent lavender light. The light dances with their every movement, and brings to the mother and child energy and grace from the angelic realm.

The mother is moved to sit closer to the plant, and begins to sing a lullaby in honor and gratitude for the graces bestowed. The lavender plant begins to move gracefully with the melody, aligning itself with the energies of the mother and child. It is this song that activates the healing properties of the plant. Whenever you stumble across some lavender, look to see if it is dancing. You might just hear its lullaby!

The Spiritual and Emotional Properties

Call on the spirit of lavender when you are recovering from a broken heart; it brings happiness when there is misery. Put sprigs of lavender around you to attract your life partner; it generates good fortune. Lavender is healing, offering life and light to your heart and creating laughter and cheer. Call on this plant spirit to bring joy to babies and children.

Lavender nourishes your energy field, and carries a high vibration of spiritual energy. It aligns the heart chakras of partners for eternity. Placing lavender plants around you will help you communicate with your deceased loved ones— beings who have crossed over use lavender as a doorway into this reality, and are drawn by its fragrant smell. In general, lavender is an excellent tool in healing rips and tears in the energy field, and can help to heal unresolved karmic issues and past incarnations.

The Physical Healing Properties

Lavender is excellent for tonifying the lymphatic system; take 2 drops of the essence in water per day. It is also helpful for soothing sinus inflammation; add a few drops of the essence to warmed olive oil and massage it onto inflamed areas.

Lavender can assist in the healing of a mild burn. Forty-eight hours after receiving the burn, crush fresh lavender flowers and infuse them into a mixture of 1 part almond oil and 2 parts grape-seed oil. Massage this lightly onto the affected area.

For healing intestinal yeast, or a rash due to fungal infection, or other rashes due to dampness and mold exposure, take 3 drops of lavender essence per day under the tongue as needed.

Lavender strengthens the kidneys, adrenal glands, and liver. Mix the essence with jojoba oil and massage it over the area of concern.

For regulating the spleen and pancreas, make an oil from almond oil, fresh violet flowers, a touch of honey, and drops of lavender essence; massage this onto the spleen and pancreas.

To alleviate the discomfort of indigestion, make a compress of fresh or dried lavender flowers and fresh or dried rosemary herb (do this by moistening the plant parts and placing them between layers of folded cotton cloth). Massage the stomach area with warmed olive oil, and then place the compress on the stomach for 10–15 minutes.

To reduce menstrual bloating, massage a mixture of drops of the essence and jojoba oil onto the pelvic area. Lavender is also useful in healing vaginal yeast infections; make a compress using the fresh or dried herb, moistened with warm water, and place it over pubic bone for 20 minutes. It is beneficial to first massage the area with warmed St. John's wort oil.

For bladder infections and toxicity in the bladder, massage the area with warmed wheat germ oil, and then place a compress of fresh or dried lavender over the pubic bone for 20-minute intervals. Putting a heating pad over the compress increases the healing effect.

For eye strain and discomfort, make a compress using just fresh lavender leaves and place it on top of the eyes for 10-minute intervals.

Lemon Balm
Plant Spirit Prayer

....

Fly, little fairy, as fast as you can, and bring magic to each lemon balm with the stroke of your hand. Using your wand, filled with God's grace, make nectar of its leaves for the entire human race.

....

Lemon Balm
(Melissa officinalis)

My Experience with This Plant Spirit

When I call on the spirit of lemon balm, a tiny, effervescent fairy comes whizzing by me. She is a delicate but strong-willed spirit, and carries a wand of magic. She stands guard at the lemon balm plant and has many messengers to help her. One of them is the royal queen bee, who travels from leaf to leaf listening to the healing wishes of those who seek lemon balm's medicine. Upon hearing the messages, the bee calls for the fairy's assistance. The fairy manifests her presence by skipping from each leaf. When she taps them with her magic wand, the healing properties of lemon balm are activated.

The Spiritual and Emotional Properties

Call on the spirit of lemon balm to help you overcome your fear of being in the world or of walking in your own shoes. Lemon balm can give you that courage. It also works to heal injustice, and helps those who believe life is unfair to see the broader picture. It gives you the strength to persevere when fighting for a good cause, or to work through unjust and unfair treatment. If a part of a person's life force is taken from them, the spirit of lemon balm will help to soothe that soul.

Lemon balm helps you maintain mental and emotional strength, so that you can overcome the fatigue associated with mental and emotional challenges. It helps the "givers" in life learn to receive, and assists in healing the energy around heartache. Call on the spirit of lemon balm when you are making amends with your children. Lemon balm also carries the energy of spiritual communion, and thus can bring people together for a spiritual purpose. It can help you aspire to the spiritual life.

The Physical Healing Properties

Lemon balm is excellent for healing the energetic effects on the lungs of smoking. Take 4 drops of the essence in water a few times a day.

For lung congestion and phlegm associated with bronchitis, pneumonia, and coughs, take 10–20 drops of lemon balm essence in water a few times a day, and also massage a mixture of drops of the essence and warmed wheat germ oil over the lung area.

For head congestion, inflammation in sinus membranes, and ear congestion, add drops of the essence to your bath water. Also make an oil from the fresh or dried flowers and apricot kernel oil, and massage it around various areas of the head and face.

For phlegm in the throat, make a mixture of olive oil, St. John's wort oil, and drops of the essence, and massage it onto the throat area.

Lemon balm acts as a cooling agent when there is too much heat in the digestive system; place drops of the essence in almond oil, and massage this mixture onto the stomach. It also is an excellent stress alleviator and can help you feel calmer; place a drop of the essence under your tongue when you're feeling a little overwhelmed.

Lemon balm stimulates the flow of the intestines and rectum and therefore assists in relieving constipation. Make a mixture of drops of the essence and warmed olive oil, and massage it onto your lower back after bathing.

To stimulate kidney and adrenal function, make a mixture of almond oil and drops of lemon balm essence, and massage it onto your kidney and adrenal area.

Lemon balm is also known for aiding physical and mental stamina and alleviating fatigue. Place a few drops of the essence under your tongue, or have lots of lemon balm plants around your home.

For muscle spasms in the uterine area, make a mixture of almond oil, St. John's wort oil, and drops of the essence and massage it onto the affected area.

To increase overall circulation, add drops of the essence to your bath water, or make an infusion of the flowers and drink it.

Lemon balm is also excellent in working with allergies that arise from airborne organisms. Drink a tea made from an infusion of the flowers, or take drops of the essence under the tongue upon waking.

LICORICE
PLANT SPIRIT PRAYER

....

Harmony of spirit, harmony of creation ... performed by the hands of
greatness and instilled in splendor.
Heal us with thy sounds and create the space for
hope, healing, and God to manifest in all.

....

Licorice
(Glycyrrhiza glabra)

My Experience with This Plant Spirit

When I call on the spirit of licorice, a great being appears before me. He is a very easygoing spirit. He carries an old guitar whose strings are worn and tired with age. He has played this guitar ever since his life on earth, and took it with him when he crossed over.

His earth life had been a very poor one. He went around with only his guitar and the clothes on his back, eating whatever food was given to him. But you wouldn't have known this by the expression on his face. His music helped him keep his faith in God, and in humanity, alive. He never stopped trusting, even though he wasn't really supported in his physical existence. He always said that it was okay; he trusted in the land and in God to take care of him always.

While taking long walks in the woods and on the beaches, he would stop to rest, strumming his guitar as he lay on the ground. Many times, he would unintentionally lie near a licorice plant. Over time, he formed a special bond with this plant and would strum his guitar every time he came upon one. The licorice plants took a fancy to him, too. They would light up every time he came by. When the time came for him to leave the earth, they were saddened and hoped to stay connected with him.

One day, music from the sky came down upon them, and they recognized the strum of those old guitar strings. Their old friend had returned—and continues to imbue the licorice plants with their magical healing qualities.

The Spiritual and Emotional Properties

Call on the spirit of licorice to heal those who have been emotionally or physically wounded in wars; licorice brings peace to veterans who have suffered physical loss. It also offers comfort and nurturing to those who have no family, and to those who are outcasts from society. Licorice helps people suffering from devastating illness, which our society looks down upon, to find peace. It helps to heal the energies surrounding a difficult child labor and birthing.

On a larger scale, licorice can work with the energies of societal and cultural issues—call on the spirit of the plant to heal the hearts of the despondent, the poor, and the oppressed. It can heal the spiritual energies around present-day slavery. In prisons, licorice fosters the energy of hope, support, and transformation for those who want to turn their lives around, and tends to the karmic energy of all societal abuses. Licorice also heals the energies around grievances in past lives, and offers resolution.

The Physical Healing Properties

Licorice is an excellent energy booster for the body. Place a few drops of the essence under your tongue.

For breathing difficulties and asthma, take 4 drops of licorice essence in water upon waking. Also massage a mixture of drops of the essence and warmed olive oil onto your chest after bathing.

To stimulate the kidneys and adrenals, make a mixture from drops of the essence and almond oil, and massage it onto the area after bathing.

Licorice clears inflammation of the sinuses, lungs, and breathing passages; place 10 drops of the essence in warmed water and sip slowly. You can also make an oil from licorice leaves and warmed olive oil; massage it onto the chest and sinus area before retiring.

To stimulate digestion and the liver, massage a mixture of drops of the essence and avocado oil onto those areas before retiring.

To help with morning sickness, place 2 drops of the essence in warm water and drink it in the morning.

Licorice is helpful for removing bladder toxicity. Make a compress of licorice leaves (moisten them with a little warm water and place them between folded layers of cotton cloth). Place this compress on top of the bladder area for 20-minute intervals. It is beneficial to massage the area first with a little warmed almond oil, and then place a heating pack on top of the compress. This is best done in the early evening.

LILAC
PLANT SPIRIT PRAYER

....

O love, pure love…
Be still my heart…
Nourish my heart with everlasting bliss and the blessings of the most
high. Bring forth union, of body, mind, and spirit, of myself, and with
each other. I place my soul within the gentleness of your tiny petals and
entrust the well-being of my heart's journey to your graces.

....

Lilac
(Syringa vulgaris)

My Experience with This Plant Spirit

When I call on the spirit of lilac, a beautiful, innocent young woman, dressed in shimmering white, appears to me. Her arms dance with subtle movements of grace, and she moves her feet in harmony with the gentle sounds of the wind. She saunters around the lilac bush, enchantedly picking its flowers, her dress flowing and catching on the branches. She is completely filled with joy and contentment.

Lilac is about be joined in spiritual union with another, and this fills her being with radiant love—a love that emanates so powerfully from her heart that it touches each and every lilac flower she passes. As she dances by the blossoms, she imbues them with grace, serenity, and everlasting content, and blesses all those who call on the plant for assistance. Henceforth, all unions of body, mind, and spirit, whether to oneself or to one another, shall have the special blessing of the lilac bush.

The Spiritual and Emotional Properties

Lilac is symbolic of transition, and honors rites of passage for both men and women. Call on the spirit of this wonderful plant when you are experiencing changes in your life. Lilac can energetically assist a woman as she transitions through menopause. This special time in life should be blessed by the lilac bush, as it helps to integrate the physical, emotional, and spiritual changes women undergo.

Lilac is also the flower of romance. Call on it to help bring the spark back into your relationship, or to assist in finding romance—lilac is wonderful in helping to attract that special someone. Lilac blesses wedding days and marriages, and brings luck to the bride and groom. It honors the sacred union between two people and helps rekindle that energy. It also blesses friendship.

Call on lilac when you are missing someone, as it helps soothe the heart. It can comfort and assuage the grief of those who have just lost their life partner to death. It has a special relationship to grandparents, and its spirit can be called upon in healing those relationships. It can also be called upon to communicate with animals, and calm them when they are in distress. The lilac flower offers much contentment and fulfillment.

The Physical Healing Properties

Lilac is excellent for healing the energies around pneumonia, bronchitis, and chest colds. Make an oil of fresh or dried flowers, with equal parts warmed almond oil and olive oil, and massage it onto the chest.

For loss of circulation in the extremities, mix a few drops of lilac essence with olive oil, and massage it into the affected area. To bring warmth to the body when it is cold, take a few drops of essence under your tongue.

Lilac also improves circulation in the lymphatic system. Add a few drops of the essence into warmed wheat germ oil and massage it onto your body.

For energetically dispersing candida and intestinal yeast, take 10–15 drops of lilac essence daily, under the tongue.

To detoxify and tonify the gallbladder, make a compress using fresh or dried flowers. Moisten the leaves with a little warmed wheat germ oil and place them between layers of folded cotton cloth. Place the compress on the gall bladder area for 20 minutes.

To detoxify and tonify the kidneys, make an oil from almond oil and fresh or dried lilac flowers, and massage it onto the kidney area.

Lilac can help with heavy menses; massage a mixture of almond oil and a few drops of the essence onto the pelvic area.

Lilac is an excellent hormone regulator. It helps to alleviate some of the symptoms associated with menopause, such as irritability, mood swings, and hot flashes. Take 8–10 drops of the essence in water, one to three times a day. Be sure to tune in to the amount, or dosage, you need—each woman's body and energy system is different and calls for a different amount. Always start out with once a day, and see how your body works with the lilac essence.

For a vaginal yeast infection, take 3 drops of the essence three times a day, under the tongue.

Lilac also assists in regulating the functions of the pancreas. Make a compress of fresh or dried flowers, moistened with olive oil and played between layers of folded cotton cloth, and place it over the pancreas for 10 minutes. When fresh or dried flowers are not available, use lilac essence. This will assist in healing the energy surrounding blood sugar imbalances.

Marshmallow
Plant Spirit Prayer

....

Divine Will, assist me in harnessing the innate power of my true and authentic self. Help hold, in my vision, my destiny, and give me the courage to manifest it in physical reality.

....

Marshmallow
(Althaea officinalis)

My Experience with This Plant Spirit

When I call on the spirit of marshmallow, many sages and mystics appear from the ethers. These spirits spend their time watching over the individual paths and journeys of human beings. They gently offer guidance and assistance when needed, subtly working with the spiritual energies surrounding a person's destiny. For example, they often help us when we get in our own way of the highest good unfolding for us. They usually do all this without our awareness of it; they are our secret spiritual helpers.

Every time these wise beings assist one of us, they grow a marshmallow plant on earth to remind us to keep aligned with the will of our highest selves. When you use the plant for healing purposes, remember that you are also receiving the energies of the miraculous endeavors of these sages and mystics of old.

The Spiritual and Emotional Properties

Call on the spirit of marshmallow when you are feeling overwhelmed by circumstances and not able to control what is happening in your life. It will bring you ease, comfort, and an understanding of the energy that is unfolding. Marshmallow is good for protection against negative energies and influences, and when you can't figure out things, marshmallow is excellent for working through your confusion to discover what makes sense. If you have lost your sense of physical direction, marshmallow will help you to get where you need to go. Also call on the spirit of marshmallow to help heal regrets. It is even helpful in healing the regrets of souls who are still wandering the ethers with pain in their hearts.

Marshmallow is excellent for helping to create structure and balance in your life. When you have to ground an idea in physical reality, marshmallow holds the space for that and fosters motivation and personal will. It gives you the energy to complete tasks, and fosters a sense of authority, personal purpose, and power. Call on the spirit of marshmallow to help you fulfill your soul's destiny.

The Physical Healing Properties

Marshmallow tonifies and strengthens the digestive system and stomach chi; take 4 drops of the essence in water upon waking. It is also good for strengthening the colon and for relieving the inflammation of hemorrhoids; steep marshmallow leaves in warmed olive oil for an hour or so, and massage it on the lower part of the back and around the rectal area.

Marshmallow improves circulation, Mix drops of the essence with almond oil and massage it onto the body after bathing.

To improve brain function and bring clarity to your mental state, place marshmallow plants around you and place a drop of the essence under your tongue upon retiring.

To energetically clear and dispel parasites and worms in the digestive tract, place a few drops of marshmallow essence in warmed water and drink it as a tea before retiring. Also make a compress with marshmallow leaves. Moisten the leaves with a little warmed water and put them between layers of folded cotton cloth. Place the compress on the stomach for 20-minute intervals. This is best done in the early evening before eating a large meal.

Marshmallow is excellent in assisting the healing of some types of skin rashes, wounds, and sores. Make an oil from marshmallow leaves, lemon balm flowers, and almond oil. Massage it onto the skin as needed. Do not use this on open wounds or sores that are bleeding.

To cleanse the gallbladder, massage the area first with warmed wheat germ oil, then make a compress using marshmallow leaves. Place the compress on the gallbladder area for 20 minutes.

When the blood sugar level is too high, marshmallow can help to bring it down by balancing the energies of the spleen and pancreas. Mix drops of the essence with warmed olive oil and massage it onto the area of the spleen and pancreas.

Marshmallow is also a good remedy for healing ulcers. Make a mixture using warmed olive oil, apricot kernel oil, drops of marshmallow essence, and a few drops of lavender essence. Massage this onto the stomach area after bathing.

MOTHERWORT
PLANT SPIRIT PRAYER

....

Rejoice, O noble one! For the kingdom of heaven is upon us.
In your glory, may miracles of God abound everywhere.

....

Motherwort
(Leonurus cardiaca)

My Experience with This Plant Spirit

When I call on the spirit of motherwort, I see a vision of many spirits playing their trumpets, waiting for a special being to join them. They announce her entrance with songs from the heavens, and upon the last note, a regal being appears in all her glory. She is a queen in the spirit world, one who knows exactly what her purpose and mission is. She is ready and willing to perform her duties. As the trumpets continue to blare, she raises her hands and delegates responsibilities to all those who serve her, all those who perform their duties on behalf of human consciousness.

This magnificent spirit works in the energetic field of human evolution, in the spiritual dimension, and creates many miracles on a daily basis. She doesn't wait to be asked for help—she can see where her assistance is needed and facilitates the healing. Every time she does this, she grows a motherwort plant on the earth plane. When using the plant for medicinal purposes, know that you are receiving the energy of the miracle performed by this noble spirit!

The Spiritual and Emotional Properties

Motherwort protects the soul force of humanity. It acts as a guide and directs the spirit, holding space for the soul's evolutionary growth. It bestows graces upon humanity and gives direction to individual's lives. It can help keep you on your path, aligned with God, and will continue to guide you throughout life.

Call on the spirit of this plant to nurture the family unit as a whole, since motherwort is known for bringing grace to the family. It protects babies in the spirit world as they get ready to incarnate into the physical reality, and heals the spirits of abandoned children and children who are lost to drugs, violence, and abuse. Call on the spirit of motherwort to heal the souls of those who are homeless.

The Physical Healing Properties

Motherwort is a very powerful plant when it comes to the spiritual healing of physical ailments. It can be used to heal the energies surrounding many autoimmune illnesses that affect brain and nervous system functioning, such as Lou Gehrig's disease and Parkinson's Disease.

Motherwort heals the energies surrounding brain aneurysms. Call on the spirit of the plant, place many plants around the patient, and also take a few drops of the essence in water upon waking.

It is also excellent in healing the energy around a heart attack or stroke. Placing plants around the patient is a wonderful remedy, as is placing 2 drops of motherwort essence under the tongue upon retiring. Placing a compress of motherwort leaves on the heart area also helps to heal the energy; moisten the leaves with a little warmed water and fold them between layers of cotton cloth. Gently place the compress on the heart area for 20-minute intervals. This is best done in the evening.

To heal the energies around tumors of the liver, spleen, pancreas, lymphatic system, intestines, and colon, make an oil from motherwort leaves, olive oil, and St. John's wort oil, and massage the warmed oil over the needed areas.

To heal the energy around stomach ulcers and ailments, make a compress by moistening motherwort leaves with a generous amount of warmed almond oil and placing the leaves between layers of folded cotton cloth. Place the compress on the stomach area for 15-minute intervals. Adding direct heat by using a heating pad is very beneficial.

Motherwort is also helpful in healing the energetic trauma of physical injuries that directly relate to the spine. Make an oil from the leaves, almond oil, and St. John's wort oil, and massage it onto the spine; do this after bathing.

Motherwort also induces rest. Take a few drops of the essence in water upon retiring and sip slowly.

If you are about to undergo major surgery, call on the spirit of motherwort to protect and heal you. To heal the scar tissue that manifests in the energy field after surgery, make an oil from a few drops of motherwort essence and olive oil, and massage it directly onto the mature scar tissue.

Motherwort can heal the energy around a heart murmur. Massage a little almond oil, with a few drops of the essence added, directly onto the heart and chest area.

To heal the energy around muscle apathy, mix drops of motherwort essence with almond oil and massage it onto the body after bathing.

MUGWORT
PLANT SPIRIT PRAYER

....

We call on you, ancestors of the earth and sky. Hear our prayers.
We need your medicine to heal our people and Mother Earth.
We thirst for wholeness. We hunger for nourishment. Carry us in your
womb as we walk this earth. Protect us from harm. Feed our children.
And when we are ready to come home to the Great Spirit in the sky,
carry us on your wings and fly.

....

Mugwort
(Artemisia vulgaris)

My Experience with This Plant Spirit

When I call on the spirit of mugwort, a medicine man comes toward me and sits in the dirt around a blazing fire. He is chanting, and holding a piece of mugwort plant cupped in his hands. He rocks back and forth over the fire while drawing the plant to his mouth and forehead, each time saying a prayer for the earth. He then takes his hand and circles it above the fire. This is to symbolize the cycle of life, of birth and death, of completion.

Invoking special prayers for the mugwort plant, the medicine man calls on the ancestors of the earth and sky to help instill it with the power of medicinal and spiritual healing properties. He makes an offering and places the mugwort into the fire, a gifting for the healing of humanity.

The Spiritual and Emotional Properties

Call on the spirit of mugwort to walk hand-in-hand with you through life, since it is the plant of journeying. It can be used when you want to motivate yourself, and helps create the desire needed to live on the earth plane. It can also be used to cross over into the spirit world. Call on mugwort to heal spirits who are lost and still wandering in other dimensional realities; it helps them find their way back home. It is also used for spiritual protection, and for clearing negative influences from an individual's energy field.

Mugwort aids in a safe journey when one is in the process of dying. It is also called upon for bringing in good harvest and protecting the children. It is a very powerful spiritual plant.

Mugwort can help to increase your sexual desire toward your partner, and also is excellent in helping people heal from sexual trauma—it gently integrates the soul pieces during recovery, helping to make the soul whole. It likewise helps with the trauma of violence; call on this plant spirit when you have suffered physical injury. It can assist in recovering from alcoholic abuse as well, by helping substance users gather strength to work through their issues.

The Physical Healing Properties

Mugwort is excellent for clearing energetic mucus from the body. Place a few drops of the essence in water and drink it upon waking.

For dryness of the mouth, lungs and chest, mix drops of the essence with warmed almond oil, and massage it onto the chest and lung area.

For fluid in the ears from colds and sinus problems, place 2 drops of mugwort essence in 1 tablespoon of warmed olive oil, and place it in the ears.

Mugwort is useful if you are suffering from indigestion or weak digestion. First, massage the stomach area with warmed avocado oil, then take fresh mugwort leaves and place them on the stomach for an hour.

For sore eyes due to allergies, make a compress by moistening mugwort leaves with a little warm water and placing them between layers of folded cotton cloth. Place the compress on the eyes for 10-minute intervals.

For fluid retention associated with urinary tract infections and incontinence, massage castor oil onto the lower abdominal region and then place fresh mugwort leaves on top. When fresh leaves are not available, make a compress using the dried herb moistened with olive oil.

For stiffness in the joints, lower back pain, and kidney discomfort, combine olive oil and a generous dosage of the essence, and massage the warmed oil onto the affected areas.

For menstrual discomfort, make an infusion of equal parts olive oil and fresh or dried mugwort, add a tablespoon of crushed rosemary, and massage it onto the pelvis area.

For minor cuts, scrapes, and mosquito bites, mix equal parts olive oil and crushed, fresh, or dried mugwort, add ½ teaspoon of bentonite clay, and place the resulting paste on the affected area. Do not use this on open wounds.

Mullein
Plant Spirit Prayer

....

*O gentleness, O wonder, O God's creation, bring forth
your sunshine, your ray of hope. Manifest through the glory of God
your eternal presence and, unto us, shine in the light of angel's wings.*

....

Mullein
(Verbascum thapsus)

My Experience with This Plant Spirit

When I call on the spirit of mullein, a gentle female voice comes to me. She has no form; she is just light. The energy of her voice is one of mystery and haste, for she is very busy being caretaker of the plant kingdom. She tells me that she is the keeper of the mullein plant, the protectorate of its life force. She watches over all of Mother Earth, our Garden of Eden, and brings sunshine and creates harmony within the plant world. Traveling from one plant to another, she spreads her nourishment.

When I first asked this plant spirit for assistance, she answered my call by appearing in the form of a ladybug sitting atop a mullein leaf. She does not draw attention to herself... she brings her medicine and then quickly goes on her way, to where she is needed next.

The Spiritual and Emotional Properties

Call on this plant spirit for support and encouragement. Mullein is helpful when you are in a constant state of worry or feeling overwhelmed; when you think you can't make it through the day, the spirit will help alleviate your stress. Mullein can heal strife and conflict within the family unit, and encourages forgiveness when there is anger.

Mullein honors the connection when loved ones are far away or separated; call on the spirit of this plant if your loved ones are missing or if little children wander off and become lost. Mullein can help you feel safe in this world, and assists in combatting boredom and fostering excitement.

Mullein can be called upon to increase your connection to, and faith in, a Higher Power. It brings magic and surprises to your life. As well as helping to maintain a healthy connection between your lower and higher selves, it keeps you aligned with Spirit.

The Physical Healing Properties

Mullein is excellent for healing the energies around asthma, lung infections, bronchitis, and shallow breathing. Take 20–30 drops of the essence in water per day.

For lethargy, place the plant near you at night while you sleep.

For healing the energy around multiple sclerosis, drink tea made from an infusion of mullein leaves. For weakness in the legs, mix drops of mullein essence and rosemary oil and massage it onto the legs.

For emphysema, take 10 drops of the essence per day, and massage an oil of crushed mullein leaves and warmed olive oil onto the chest.

Mullein is also useful when dealing with skin problems. For a baby's diaper rash, mix a few drops of the essence with olive oil and massage it onto the affected area. For prickly heat and other inflamed rashes, make a paste of fresh crushed mullein leaves, crushed juniper berries, and olive oil; place this mixture on the rash for 20-minute intervals a few times per day.

For burning skin from environmental pollutants, mix mullein essence with almond oil and massage it generously into the skin. For eczema, psoriasis, and other skin rashes due to digestive disturbances, make a paste using bentonite clay, mullein leaves, and olive oil, and place it on the skin for 10–15 minute intervals once a day.

For arthritis, make the same paste as above and leave on the inflamed area for an hour wrapped in cotton cloth. This is best done in the evening before retiring.

For mercury and chemical toxicity, kidney toxicity, and environmental toxins in the body, drink an infusion of mullein leaves.

NETTLES
PLANT SPIRIT PRAYER

....

O loving kindness, drench the fires of our bitterness and scorn.
Weep not, for the ills of the human heart can only be appeased by your
unbounded, gracious love.

....

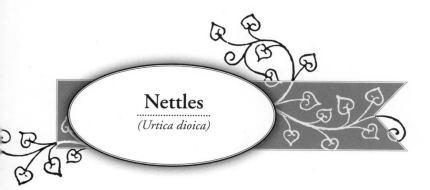

Nettles
(Urtica dioica)

My Experience with This Plant Spirit

When I call upon the spirit of nettles, I see not one but two spirits hiding among the leaves. They are the fairies of this wondrous plant, and their arms swing to the rhythm of their stinging tails, which follow along behind them. One fairy is male and the other is female. The male is the bitter one; feelings of being unwanted and unloved permeate his being. He is angry at the world, refusing to believe in goodness and loving kindness. He sits upon the leaves and instills his scorn into the plant, in an effort to make it as unlovable as he.

The female fairy holds the light of the nettle plant. She is a gentle being, loving, compassionate, and trusting of the world. She radiates loving kindness into the nettle plant, helping it keep its energies in balance. She will stay with the nettle and imbue it with love as long as the other fairy is there. She also keeps her heart open toward the other fairy, constantly sending him unconditional love and acceptance.

It is this balance of the two fairies that gives the nettle plant its wondrous healing abilities.

The Spiritual and Emotional Properties

Call on the spirit of nettles to assist you when you are thinking negative thoughts, or feeling negative emotions that aren't serving your highest good. The nettle plant helps to heal the energy around bitterness and scorn. It dissipates vengeful thoughts, and works to heal jealousy and envy. It also can help to bring you out of a state of selfishness or self-absorption, and fosters empathy for others.

Nettles are excellent when working with those who are possessive, obsessive, and controlling. The plant can bring about a change of heart in a person. It is also excellent for grounding, and will align your source of power with that of Divine Right. It is useful in bringing some resolution to marital conflict and divorce.

The Physical Healing Properties

Nettles are excellent for sinus and lung congestion due to allergens, helping to build up the immune system's natural defenses. Take 5 drops of the essence under the tongue upon waking.

For bronchitis, make a mixture of nettle essence and warmed wheat germ oil, and massage it on the chest area upon retiring.

To help energetically clear the lymphatic system, take 3–6 drops of the essence in water, two to three times a day. Nettles also build strength in the body; place a drop of the essence under your tongue when you are feeling fatigued.

Nettles are an overall blood strengthener and builder; drink a tea of the leaves, or place 5–7 drops of the essence in warm water. The plant is also excellent for anemia and replenishing iron; you can make a tea of the leaves for this as well, or place a few drops of the essence under the tongue upon waking.

When a woman is menstruating heavily, nettles help with the loss of minerals from the blood. Taking 10–15 drops of the essence while menstruating is a good remedy.

Nettles also help to alleviate stomach acid, and work to calm digestive problems. Make a mixture of the essence and almond oil, and massage it onto the stomach after bathing.

To strengthen the liver, make a mixture of nettle essence and wheat germ oil, and massage it onto the liver area. Nettles can cleanse the gall bladder and stomach as well; drink a tea of fresh nettle leaves before retiring.

Nettles help heal the energy around arthritis. Take 5–10 drops of the essence in water per day upon waking.

To cleanse the intestines and colon, take dried nettle leaves and simmer them (covered) for 20 minutes. Slowly sip this tea in the evening time.

The nettle plant has stinging hairs on each leaf. It is advisable to use gloves when collecting the plant, unless you are gathering it very early in the springtime. When brewed to make a tea, however, the stingers in the leaves become deactivated.

POKE
PLANT SPIRIT PRAYER

....

Great Creator and Spirit of the Buffalo, we surrender to your power-
ful medicine. We stand here before you, seeking guidance and direction.
Bring to us your wisdom, Great Spirit, so that we may follow in the
trails you leave behind. Show us the way, for we are your children.

....

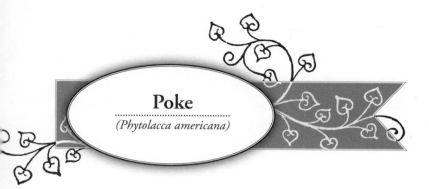

Poke
(Phytolacca americana)

My Experience with This Plant Spirit

When I call on the spirit of poke, a beautiful, dark-skinned Native American woman comes forth. She is adorned with leather buffalo hides and intricate, blue and pink beadwork. Her hands are outstretched, as if to embrace the mysteries of life. She is surrounded by flames of red fire that burst from the earth, crying out for the wounds of humanity.

The woman calls out to the white buffalo. There, appearing before her, is a sacred white buffalo of enormous stature and presence. Markings of deep red, painted on its body, symbolize the sufferings of the mother. This magnificent creature brings with it all the medicines necessary for healing the spirit of the earth's people. It prances around angrily, setting its hoofs upon the flames and giving the human race's anger to the fire for purification.

After sharing the wisdom it received from the ritual, the buffalo returns to its source, leaving behind a powerful poke plant. The Native woman sits near the plant and makes an offering of a strand of her hair. She thanks the spirit for its assistance.

The Spiritual and Emotional Properties

Call on the spirit of poke to help bring good fortune and luck into your life. Poke can also bring warmth and love into your heart, and help to clear your mind. It alleviates fear and anxiety, promoting a deep sense of faith and trust in yourself and your purpose. Poke also brings calmness and helps to heal the spirit when it is broken. Call on this plant spirit to soothe your baby when it cries incessantly.

Poke assists in aligning an individual with their soul's intention. It can be used for strength, especially when you are making leaps and bounds in your personal growth. It is good for protection when traveling, and helpful in integrating your emotional and mental faculties when there is a lot of confusion.

Ask poke to help you call upon your own spirit guides and helpers; it is a very sacred plant. It can be used to induce trancelike or waking-dream states of consciousness for healing purposes. It is also brings clarity to your intuitive sense, and is useful in establishing healthy energetic boundaries between a parent and child. Poke is used to honor the ancestors and elders who have come before us. It assists in the healing of the planetary consciousness.

The Physical Healing Properties

Do not harvest the poke plant for this essence (see caution, below). Do not use when pregnant or nursing.

Poke is useful for soothing throat irritation; mix drops of the essence with wheat germ oil, and massage it on the throat area. For shallow breathing, mix a few drops of the essence with warmed olive oil, and massage it onto the chest area.

It is very helpful for hemorrhoids. Mix drops of poke essence and warmed olive oil, and massage it on the outside of the rectal area.

For intestinal parasites, add 2–6 drops of the essence in warm water and drink sparingly—poke is a very strong vibrational medicine. The tea can also be taken for intestinal and stomach cleansing.

For muscle soreness, make a mixture of almond oil, drops of poke essence, and lavender leaves, and massage it onto the sore areas.

To heal the energies around strong influenza and tuberculosis, make a tea of 8–10 drops of the essence and hot water, adding a touch of honey and lemon.

For anxiety and nervousness, take 4–6 drops of poke essence 3 times a day until the anxiety dissipates.

Call on the spirit of the plant to address mental illness and dissociative disorders. Also call on poke to assist with Down's syndrome and mental retardation. It will help to rebalance and recirculate the energy around the head.

For serious illnesses, the poke plant spirit can assist with energetic and environmental sensitivities, and helps to strengthen the patient's energy field.

Caution:

Many parts of the poke plant are mildly poisonous and are not for consumption. Poke is to be handled by experienced practitioners and foragers only. For your own safety, do not harvest or use any part of the poke plant when making this plant spirit essence. Use the suggested prayer, meditate on the plant, and call on the plant spirit to imbue the essence with its healing properties.

Pulsatilla
Plant Spirit Prayer

....

*O Holy of Holies, we beseech thee to embrace our prayers with the pow-
ers of Spirit, with the essence of God. We surrender before your discern-
ment and ask for the grace of healing. We ask that our prayers be carried
to heaven upon the wings of the hummingbird, and return answered
according to the will of the highest good.*

....

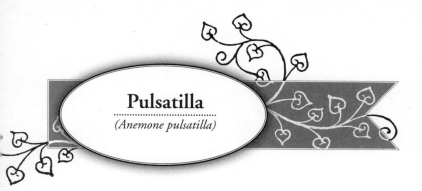

Pulsatilla
(Anemone pulsatilla)

My Experience with This Plant Spirit

When I call on the spirit of pulsatilla, a darling little hummingbird swoops down from amidst the trees. With its vibrant fuschia markings, it flutters aimlessly around the beautiful purple petals of the pulsatilla plant. It sticks its long beak into the yellow center of the flower, then hastily flies off as if carrying something in its mouth. As it heads into the clouds, I realize that the hummingbird is carrying a prayer that someone placed within the loving embrace of pulsatilla's petals.

The clouds begin to pull apart, making a passageway for the little bird. The sun shines ever so brightly. The sky is filled with brilliant rays of golden yellow light, and out of the ethers appear two magnificent hands, cupped and ready to receive the offering the hummingbird brings. The bird gently places the prayer into the hands of this holy one, where it is read with much compassion.

If you listen closely enough, you will hear the voice belonging to these gifted hands—it is the voice of the miraculous St. Francis of Assisi. St. Francis answers the prayer and then returns it to the hummingbird's beak. The little bird returns to the flower, and places the prayer gently where he found it.

Every time you see a hummingbird, remember your prayers are being answered.

The Spiritual and Emotional Properties

Call on the spirit of pulsatilla to learn compassion and how to avoid judging yourself and others, as well as how to love yourself wholly and with complete acceptance. Also call on pulsatilla if you are feeling regret about your life; it can help you understand the larger picture of why things unfold the way they do. Pulsatilla is useful if you are feeling melancholy or discontent, and can aid in healing issues of abandonment. It also assists emotionally with the process of abortion, and works to heal the energy field from this energetic trauma.

Pulsatilla also helps a person take responsibility for their actions towards others, and in making amends with themselves around these actions. It gives us the courage to heal, fosters mutual respect in people, and nourishes and repairs friendships. Symbolic of the Christian celebration of Easter and of rebirth, pulsatilla brings new openings into one's life, representing the chance to begin anew. As the plant of resurrection, of new and everlasting life, pulsatilla is the promise of the Eternal Kingdom in the here and now, and to come. It is a flower of hope, and assists in healing deep despair.

The Physical Healing Properties

Pulsatilla is good for headaches; take 2 drops of the essence in water every hour until the pain subsides. When your energy is low and it feels like the wind got knocked out of you, take

1–3 drops of the essence under your tongue. For dizziness, just smelling the flowers will help bring your energy back to center.

Pulsatilla also helps heal the energy around chicken pox and shingles; place drops of the essence, or fresh or dried flowers, in a bath and soak. To help alleviate some of the discomfort associated with allergies to pollen, drink 1–2 drops of the essence in water upon waking.

For low blood pressure, mix a bit of pulsatilla essence with wheat germ oil, and massage it generously on the inside of your wrists, along the inside of feet, and between the breast bone.

Pulsatilla can assist in bringing on a normal menstrual flow when one is irregular. When menstruation begins, make a compress by taking fresh or dried pulsatilla flowers and leaves, moistening them with a little olive oil, and placing them between folded layers of cotton cloth. Massage the area first with warmed olive oil, then place the compress on the pelvic area for 20–30 minute intervals once a day. This is best done in the morning.

To tonify the uterus and ovaries, massage a few drops of the essence along with warmed almond oil onto your pelvic area. Pulsatilla also helps to tonify the colon; mix the fresh or dried flowers with olive oil, and massage the warmed oil onto the lower back.

Pulsatilla is excellent for anemia and low iron. Take 2 drops of the essence, along with 2 drops of nettle essence, to make an overall tonifying remedy.

It is also good for tonifying the liver. Mix wheat germ oil, castor oil, and a few drops of the essence, and massage it over the liver. Adding heat for 10 minutes or so will increase the benefits of this remedy.

Call on the spirit of pulsatilla to help balance your nervous system, or take a drop of the essence under the tongue.

RED CLOVER
PLANT SPIRIT PRAYER

....

From the time of birth to the ending of life,
may the cycle of Spirit never be broken.
May the fire of God bless us and keep holy the path we walk.

....

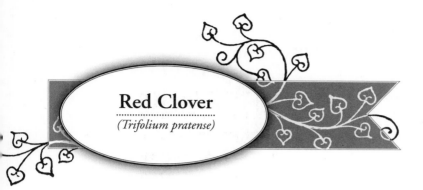

Red Clover
(Trifolium pratense)

My Experience with This Plant Spirit

When I call on the spirit of red clover, a strong and solemn male voice answers my prayer. This voice belongs to a spirit who incarnated on the earth long ago. He now exists in alternate realities in the spirit world, continuing with the work he started many centuries ago. He shows me his hands, which are very strong and powerful—the hands of a healer.

He once helped to heal many, laying his hands upon those who sought his help. He also counseled people in their troubles, and made medicines from plants to give to others. One evening, after a long day of hard work and assisting others, he sat at his washing bowl and submerged his hands into the water to cleanse himself of the energies of the day. He brought his hands, cupped with water, to his face and quenched his tired skin. Upon finishing his ritual, he noticed some markings in the water that formed a pattern.

It resembled a flame, the fire of God. The healer started to weep at God's acknowledgment of his work, and humbly thanked his Creator. He was so moved that he brought the water outside to nourish the many plants he worked with, one of which was red clover. He threw the water from the bowl over the red clover, and from that moment forward, each leaf of the plant has been marked with the symbol of the awesome fire of God. Red clover is a very powerful healing plant.

The Spiritual and Emotional Properties

Call on the spirit of red clover to help heal pain and conflict between a husband and wife. It is also useful in healing a person's relationship with their mother and father. Call on the spirit of the plant when there is great emotional distance between immediate family members, since red clover helps strengthen the family unit and bring it closer together.

Red clover provides courage when an apology is called for. It can heal anger in the heart space and helps you find forgiveness in the most challenging of situations. Red clover is about honoring—it assists you in finding a sense of honor within yourself and toward others.

Red clover can be used if you are feeling ashamed and unworthy, since it nurtures the courage you need to express yourself and share your innermost feelings. It is a plant of fortitude, and fosters determination, will, and the persistence to keep going. It encourages honesty within oneself, as well as toward others. It helps when you are feeling angst and a loss of control over things in your life, working to bring a sense of balance back. It aids you in taking responsibility for your actions—when looking for a job, call on red clover to bring you good luck. It also helps heal the energy when someone has been in a car accident.

Call on the spirit of red clover to help you reground after going through a major life change. When you need to create a new structure so that life can have a different meaning for you, red clover will energetically provide the stillness, inner strength, and clarity for you to move forward. It is a companion plant spirit, one that can always be depended upon.

The Physical Healing Properties

Red clover helps to heal the emotional energy around throat cancer. Make an oil from the fresh or dried flowers mixed with St. John's wort oil, and massage it over the throat area. The essence may be used when flowers are not available.

For sinus inflammation, mix wheat germ oil and fresh or dried red clover flowers, and massage the warmed oil over the sinus passages. To strengthen eyesight, take one drop of the essence under tongue upon waking.

To improve circulation, throw some leaves and flowers into your hot bath, or massage the body with warmed oil made from fresh or dried red clover flowers and olive oil.

Red clover can help to tonify, purify, and cleanse the blood. Take 3–6 drops of the essence under the tongue in the morning.

It also aids in healing the energy around lymphatic cancer. Take 2–4 drops of the essence per day in warmed water upon waking, and also place drops of the essence in your bath.

To combat the effects of the toxins from smoking, take 2–6 drops of the essence in water in the early afternoon. To help ease the pain of migraines, take 1 drop immediately under the tongue at the onset of the pain.

Red clover is excellent for healing the energy around the birth of a child through caesarian section. Place the plant around you at night while sleeping, and also make mix fresh or dried red clover flowers, lavender leaves, and almond oil, and massage it onto the area of the uterus.

For ectopic pregnancies, use the same oil, and massage onto the area of the uterus.

Red clover is sacred in that it nourishes the energy of the mother's breast milk while she is nursing. Just place red clover plants around you during this time!

Likewise, red clover can nourishes the mother's system on a physical and energetic level after pregnancy. Following the birth of the child, and during the first year, take 1 drop of the essence in water when needed.

To reduce the discomfort and aid in the energetic healing of breast polyps, make a mixture of red clover essence and warmed olive oil, and massage it over the breasts.

To ease lower back pain, massage a mixture of drops of the essence and almond oil over the intended area.

To assist the energetic healing of yeast infections, take 8–10 drops of red clover essence in water per day.

For detoxifying the liver and kidneys, add a few drops of the essence to castor oil and make a castor oil pack to place over the kidneys and liver as needed.

Red clover also strengthens the adrenals. Make a mixture of warmed wheat germ oil, drops of the essence, and drops of rosemary essence, and massage it onto the adrenal area.

To heal the energy surrounding general infections, take 10–20 drops of the essence in water per day. To help remove toxicity from the body, take 3–5 drops of the essence in water per day.

For worms and parasites, take 15 drops of the essence in water per day upon retiring, as needed.

Red clover is very beneficial in healing the energy of all sexually transmitted diseases, such as gonorrhea, syphilis, and hepatitis. Take 15 drops of the essence per day under the tongue upon waking. Also massage a mixture of warmed St. John's wort oil and drops of the essence onto the pubic area.

ROSEMARY
PLANT SPIRIT PRAYER

....

O Divine Mother, all loving, all knowing, ever so present.
Fill our hearts with the grace of your love. Hold us in your
tender arms. Give to us divine mercy in our suffering.
Be with us at the time of our loneliness. Show us how to be
compassionate with ourselves and with humankind.
Teach us the ways of God.

....

Rosemary
(Rosmarinus officinalis)

My Experience with This Plant Spirit

When I call on the spirit of rosemary, I hear the angelic voice of a little girl. She is soft and almost transparent in nature, and nestles among the many flowers of her world. She has always had a special relationship with her flowers, especially the rosemary bush. She is also very connected with the energy of the Divine Mother, and filled with much unconditional love to give. She frolics joyfully, with no worries or cares in the world, keeping to herself and tending to her flowers. Her love for them and for God transcends her everyday realities.

As she comes close to the rosemary bush, she stoops, her dress sweeping the dirt, and reaches out to hold a piece of rosemary tightly in her hand. She begins to talk with the bush. As she does, a magnificent ray of light emerges behind her, filled with golden-blue hues of vibrant warmth and radiance. The light embraces the little girl, and within it a form begins to take shape. The Divine Mother Mary, her arms outstretched, envelops the child and the rosemary plant, imbuing both of them with her energy. The child's heart fills with a love so expansive that tears begin to roll down her cheeks. One of the tears falls upon the rosemary bush, giving it its healing properties.

The Spiritual and Emotional Properties

Call on the spirit of rosemary to comfort yourself when you are feeling alone and lonely. It brings quietness and stillness into your life and fosters understanding. Rosemary also protects the home from intruders and is a wonderful protective force against dark and negative energies.

Rosemary is essential to the forgiveness process on many levels. It helps you heal grudges and resolve past resentments and bitterness toward others. Also call on rosemary to help you forgive your own past, and make peace with yourself around it. Rosemary will assist you in letting go and finding that place inside that can give you the courage to move on. It will aid you in reclaiming the present and opening up to whatever the future has in store for you. It will help you heal old wounds and forgive your parents.

The spirit of rosemary is very connected to the Divine Mother energy, and brings holiness to your life and to the various situations you encounter. It opens doorways into the higher self, assists you in staying present, and helps you create a vision for your future. To anoint oneself with rosemary is to be truly blessed by God.

The Physical Healing Properties

Rosemary assists in shifting the energies associated with shallow breathing and congestion in the lungs due to smoking. Infuse the fresh or dried herb in almond oil, and then massage it onto the chest area. Also take a homeopathic dosage of 2–6 drops of the essence per day.

For headaches, take 6 drops of the essence in water at the onset of the pain. For sinus trouble, mix dried or fresh rosemary and olive oil, and massage it into the affected area.

To stimulate the circulatory system, take 1 drop of rosemary essence under the tongue daily, in late morning to early afternoon.

Drinking an infusion of rosemary leaves is beneficial in lowering cholesterol. For detoxifying the liver, drink an infusion of the leaves as well.

Rosemary helps to alleviate stomach acid. When stomach acid begins to be disruptive, massage a mixture of warmed olive oil and 2–3 drops of rosemary essence onto the gastrointestinal area.

To strengthen the immune system, take a homeopathic dosage of 1–3 drops of the essence when your system feels weakened. Drinking a tea made from an infusion of the leaves will help as well.

Rosemary is also beneficial for arthritis pain. Mix almond oil with fresh rosemary leaves and massage it onto the affected areas.

To regulate blood sugar and nourish the spleen energy, mix fresh or dried rosemary, or a few drops of the essence, with warmed wheat germ oil, and massage it over the spleen and pancreas.

For sore throats, mix a bit of rosemary essence with olive oil and St. John's wort oil, and massage it over the throat area.

RUE
PLANT SPIRIT PRAYER

....

*Almighty Spirit, bring us everlasting life as we embark
on our journeys. Heal us from the ills of self and protect our souls from
harm. We ask this in accordance with divine righteousness.*

....

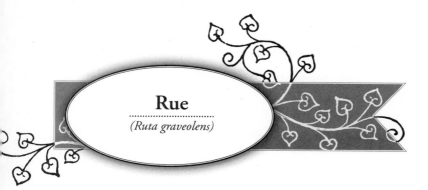

Rue
(Ruta graveolens)

My Experience with This Plant Spirit

When I call on the spirit of rue, lightning and thunder roll across the sky. No apparition appears, but an intense voice bursts forth amid the loud roars of the heavens. This is the spirit of rue. He will never show himself to humans, only to the rue plant. The rue are like his children; he nurtures them and grows them with care. Every time a request for healing is made, the spirit sends heavy rains to each rue plant, along with brilliant showers of lightning and bursts of thunder. The leaves, excited by the energies they sense, reach toward the sky, and their tips are graced by the light of this fiery and powerful spirit.

The Spiritual and Emotional Properties

Call on the spirit of rue to help with mental hysteria. Excellent in warding off evil spirits and negative energies, Rue is used to draw out spirits that have inhabited a person's body.

It is useful to call on rue when you feeling disembodied in general.

Rue can also assist in crossing over into other dimensions. It facilitates and supports medicine dreams and altered states of consciousness. Rue is a very powerful plant and should be used with care!

Rue protects babies and fetuses inside the womb from harm, and watches over those going on long journeys. In any tradition, it can be used when performing last rites on a dying person to help protect the soul as it crosses over. Many spirits of the light are drawn to rue in reverence. Rue protects the etheric realm, and strengthens the etheric field in your energy body.

The Physical Healing Properties

Do not use when pregnant or nursing.

Rue is a good blood cleanser and improves circulation. Take 4 drops of the essence in water upon waking.

It also cleanses the arteries and improves blood and oxygen flow to the heart; take a drop of the essence in water upon waking. You can also massage the heart area with warmed St. John's wort oil, then take fresh rue leaves and place them on the heart area for 10–15 minutes.

Rue can help to alleviate nausea, and also brings alkalinity to the stomach and digestive tract. Make a compress by moistening fresh rue leaves with a little warm water and placing the leaves between folded layers of cotton cloth. Leave the compress on the stomach for 20–30 minute intervals.

It draws toxins out of the liver, gall bladder, and kidneys. Massage the affected area first with a little warmed avocado oil, then take fresh rue leaves and place them on top of the affected areas.

It also balances uterine energy and improves circulation in the uterus. Mix fresh rue leaves and almond oil, and massage the warmed oil onto the pelvis.

To help heal the energy associated with rheumatoid arthritis and other joint and muscular pain, steep rue leaves in olive oil, and massage the warmed oil over painful areas of the body.

To energetically maintain homeostasis in the body and balance the endocrine system, take 2 drops of the essence under the tongue as needed.

Rue can assist in healing the energy of Lyme disease. Place rue plants around you, or place a few drops of the essence in water and sip slowly on a daily basis.

SAGE
PLANT SPIRIT PRAYER

....

Grandmother, we open our arms to take in your wisdom. Let us not be foolish in our ways. Heal us from impatience and ignorance. Help us to walk the path of righteousness with Spirit. Guide us, and help us to guide those who come after us. We pray to you, O Grandmother, that we may be made humble, to pass on your wisdom.

....

Sage
(Salvia officinalis)

My Experience with This Plant Spirit

When I call on the spirit of sage, I hear the crackling voice of an elderly woman. She is a storyteller, a wise woman, gifted with tales passed down from one generation to the next. She sits at a potting wheel; this has been one of her hobbies since she was a child. She is creating something, an object of beauty that will eventually be given to someone special.

Surrounding her are children, who come from all over to hear her stories. She shares with them the importance of listening to their elders, and talks about how pride, envy, hatred, and jealousy can cause us to lose our spirits. She communicates the importance of loving one another and sharing what Spirit gave us. Most importantly, she reminds all of us to "do unto others as you would have others do unto you."

Taking out the sage plant she has had since she was a child, she passes it around so that all the children can touch it. She tells them that it was this very sage plant that taught her everything she knows, that passed down to her all of her most prized stories. She says that each sage plant has a story to tell, and if you listen closely, you will hear it. Now that she has passed on from her earthly life, her spirit stays close to sage, wherever it grows, and helps others to hear its stories.

The Spiritual and Emotional Properties

Call on the spirit of sage when you are feeling anger or rage toward another, as it will help you heal it. In general, sage helps to clear negative thoughts you might be having by bringing the focus back to yourself. If you feel tempted to seek vengeance on another, call on sage to help you remember your spiritual self.

Sage assists in clearing evil and darkness from people, circumstances, and situations. It can help you gain insight into your shadow side, heal scorn and bitterness, and illuminate ego, self-righteousness, and pride. It helps to ease the suffering that results from envy and jealousy, especially in personal relationships. It helps to heal strife and conflict between children. Call on the spirit of sage to heal negative emotions between family members.

Sage is one of the most powerful and sacred protectors against harm and evil spirits, and can assist you in staying on your path and walking in the right direction.

The Physical Healing Properties

Do not use when pregnant.

Sage is wonderful for quenching thirst on a hot summer's day. Make an infusion of the leaves, add lemon and wildflower honey, cool it, and enjoy.

For colds and stuffy noses, take a dosage of 1–2 drops of the essence every hour until the symptoms clear.

For coughs, take 3 drops of the essence every hour until the cough subsides. For swollen glands in the throat, make an oil with fresh or dried sage and olive oil. Massage the warmed oil onto the throat area.

Sage is useful for lung congestion. Take a bit of the essence and add it to warmed wheat germ oil, and massage this onto the area of the lungs.

To strengthen the adrenals and kidneys, mix a few drops of sage essence with almond and wheat germ oils, and massage it into the kidney and adrenal areas.

For increased overall muscular strength and muscle tone, massage a mixture of olive oil and dried or fresh sage into the muscles.

To improve circulation within the digestive tract, make a compress by moistening fresh or dried sage (fresh preferred here) with warmed olive oil and placing it between layers of folded cotton cloth. Lay the compress on the stomach for 20–30 minutes. Do this late in the morning to early evening, not too soon before or after a meal.

Sage also helps ease the discomfort of menstrual cramping and with regulating the menstrual cycle. For cramps, take 2 drops of the essence in water upon waking. Do this once a day during your cycle until the cramping subsides. If your cycle is irregular, take 2 drops of the essence and mix it with almond oil; massage this onto the pelvis.

Sage also helps heal the energy around varicose veins in the legs. Infuse almond oil with fresh sage and rosemary leaves, leave it overnight when the moon is full, and massage it onto the legs for 10 days. You also need to pray to the plant spirit for help with this.

When you need to feel more grounded, call on the spirit of sage to assist. It will also help to take one drop of the essence under the tongue and place a few drops of the essence 2 inches below the belly button.

SKULLCAP
PLANT SPIRIT PRAYER

....

Rod of light, cast down upon us your invincible power of God.
Through the Holy Spirit,
manifest the truth of all things hidden and unseen.

....

Skullcap
(Scutellaria laterifolia)

My Experience with This Plant Spirit

When I call on the spirit of skullcap, a male spirit appears. He completed life on earth many years ago, but before his passing, he left many things incomplete. Therefore, from the moment he crossed over into the spirit world, he made a vow to assist others in uncovering truth in their lives and bringing light and completion to their experiences.

He stands at the threshold of the clouds, a man of great stature. He holds a staff of invincible power in his hand. He is a determined spirit, but will only help when called upon, since he acknowledges each person's free will to live their lives as they choose. When his assistance is requested, he raises his staff to the clouds and summons the winds to pull them apart. He then calls upon the skullcap plant to help in his endeavors. The plant willingly presents itself, and the spirit takes his staff and directs the winds of power to touch the plant, thereby imbuing it with its healing abilities.

The Spiritual and Emotional Properties

Call on the spirit of skullcap to help open the throat chakra, as it can give you the courage to speak. This is especially useful for those whose expression was stifled in their younger years and are striving to have a voice. Skullcap also helps to heal insecurity and shyness, the energetic trauma around deafness, and the energies around mental and physical disabilities. It can heal the energetic trauma of cerebral palsy, and works to energetically balance brain function. Skullcap also works in the etheric field by healing the spiritual pattern that allows various energies to take root in the body.

Skullcap is known to unlock and unveil secrets that have been withheld for a long time and are destructive to the spirit. It helps brings things to completion, and brings to light the unknown or hidden aspects of your life in a safe and gentle way. Call on the spirit of skullcap if you are feeling totally disconnected from Spirit due to overreliance on the intellect, distraction, emotional wounding, or loss of grounding. It can also help heal the energetic challenges around relationships between brothers and sisters.

The Physical Healing Properties

Skullcap is excellent for healing the energies around hay fever and allergies. Take 4–6 drops of the essence in water a few times daily, as needed.

For pressure headaches, make a compress by moistening skullcap leaves and placing them between layers of folded cotton cloth. Place the compress on the forehead for 20-minute intervals.

For phlegm in the throat and lungs, take a few drops of skullcap essence in water as needed. Also mix the essence into warmed almond oil and massage it onto the chest and throat area. This remedy is good if you are experiencing difficulty breathing due to allergies.

Skullcap helps to heal the energy around tonsillitis. Mix a few drops of the essence with St. John's wort oil and massage it onto the throat area.

Skullcap acts as a natural sedative. Place the plants around you when you are resting, or take a drop of the essence under your tongue.

For general irritability, take 2 drops of the essence in warmed water and sip slowly. For irritability associated with premenstrual syndrome, massage a generous amount of warmed olive oil, mixed with drops of the essence, onto the pelvis.

For uterine cramping and as a natural relaxant for the uterine muscles, place skullcap plants around you. Also, infuse skullcap leaves with almond and avocado oils and massage it onto the pelvis.

Skullcap helps relieves vaginal burning and itching that is associated with viral infections. Make a compress by moistening skullcap leaves with a little warmed olive oil and placing them between layers of folded cotton cloth. Place the compress on the pubic area for 15–20 minutes.

To alleviate the itching and toxins that come with insect bites, make a paste using a little bentonite clay, a touch of water, and some drops of skullcap essence, and place it on the affected areas. Do not use this on open sores.

ST. JOHN'S WORT
PLANT SPIRIT PRAYER

....

Divine Truth, shed for us healing waters through your many tears.
Shed for us the breath of life through your blood.
Deliver us into the grace of eternal life. Grant us peace within.

....

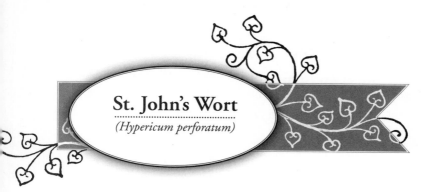

St. John's Wort
(Hypericum perforatum)

My Experience with This Plant Spirit

When I call on the spirit of St. John's wort, I see a miraculous vision of a beautiful garden filled with flowering St.
John's wort plants. Golden healing energy emanates from
them toward all living creatures in the area. The energy is so
beautiful that many deer are drawn to the garden, sitting by
the plants and sharing in their grace.

St. John's wort is sacred in that it is connected to both
St. John the Baptist and Jesus Christ. Whenever a prayer
is directed to the saint, you can find him hovering over a
St. John's wort plant. With arms outstretched and a serious
intention in his eyes, he is answering the many prayers that
come his way. Blood falls from his wrists and hands, landing
gently on the leaves of the plant. The St. John's wort then
becomes enveloped in a glowing, radiant red light. In this
act of surrendering to a higher good, it begins to shed tears
and drops of red blood from its flowers and leaves; the blood

is symbolic of the blood Christ shed for humanity. St. John's wort willingly gives itself over to Spirit, to help heal many souls on a higher level of consciousness.

As this unfolding is taking place, many creatures come and surround the holy saint and the plant, basking in the healing energy that is emanating from it.

The Spiritual and Emotional Properties

St. John's wort represents the bodhisattva, the realized being who chooses to forgo nirvana (or put off the kingdom of God) in order to help relieve the suffering of others. It brings blessings, light, and miraculous spiritual energy, creates gentleness in animals, and enhances our connection with the Divine. The plant can create miracles in life by increasing faith, and can help you turn around events in your life and become more positive when you least expect it.

St. John's wort is excellent for healing depression. Call on the spirit of this plant if you are healing from the loss of a child or experiencing any great loss in your life, as it nurtures the spirit in the heart space during overwhelming grief. It can also help you feel more assured and secure in your life. It fosters self-confidence and self-esteem, encourages awareness, and helps you see the path ahead clearly. It is an excellent protection against evil spirits.

The Physical Healing Properties

St. John's wort is excellent for healing the energy around spinal cord injuries, paralysis, and any other traumatic shock to the nervous system. Make an oil by adding St. John's wort flowers to equal amounts of almond, olive, and grape seed oils. Massage it onto the spine after bathing and before retiring.

To help to heal the pain of sciatica and to energetically help manipulate a locked sacrum, massage a mixture of warmed wheat germ oil and a few drops of St. John's wort essence onto the affected area.

For healing the energy around blocked arteries, mix St. John's wort flowers and leaves with equal amounts of grape seed and borage oils, and massage it onto the chest area.

To help heal the energy of a prolapsed uterus, lovingly massage warmed almond oil with drops of the essence onto your abdomen and pelvis.

For congestion and mucus in the throat, lungs, and gallbladder, drink a tea made from hot water, a slice of lemon, and some drops of St. John's wort essence along with a touch of red clover essence. Massaging a mixture of warmed olive oil and a bit of the essence onto the lung area is also good for congestion.

For congestion in the head and ear canals, drink a tea made from St. John's wort flowers and mullein leaves.

For headaches due to poor nutrition, place 1 drop of St. John's wort essence under the tongue at the onset of discomfort. It would also be wise to examine your nutritional habits to prevent headaches in the future.

St. John's wort gently tonifies the immune system; take 2 drops of the essence in water upon waking. It also works to energetically balance an overactive thyroid; take 5 drops of the essence in water upon retiring.

To tonify the eyesight, moisten fresh or dried leaves and flowers with water and place them between folded layers of cotton cloth. Put this compress on the eyes for 20-minute intervals.

Arranging the plant around you will induce sleep and bring calm. To help ease anxiety, place a few drops of the essence under the tongue.

VIOLET
PLANT SPIRIT PRAYER

....

*O Great Spirit, offer unto us your arms of nurturance and deliverance.
In thy holy veil, grant us peace and harmony. Send forth your light to all
those who seek your assistance, and open to us the doors of heaven.*

....

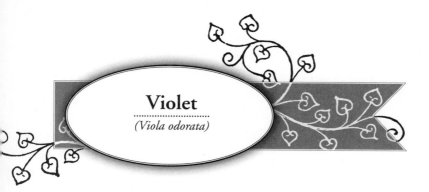

Violet
(Viola odorata)

My Experience with This Plant Spirit

When I call on the spirit of violet, a female essence appears to me. She is luminescent, surrounded by beams of violet-blue light that cradle her every shadow. She is ensconced in a flowing white robe and has somewhat androgynous features. Her hair nestles against her face and drops down her back. In her hand, she holds a beautiful white dove that carries a sprig of violet in its beak.

Upon invoking the magic and healing powers of the sprig of violet, the luminous spirit sends the dove off to bring light and peace to those in need. The sacred bird places the violet within the souls of all who have called to violet for help. She is the plant spirit of harmony.

The Spiritual and Emotional Properties

Call on the spirit of violet to bring harmony if you feel disharmony within your being. Violet is soothing and calming when you have too many thoughts, and encourages a feeling of wholeness and centeredness. It also brings gentleness and the energy of simplicity to life when things become overwhelming. It can even create joy and glee in your life.

Violet is sacred in that it fosters compatibility, cooperation, and peace among people. It manifests light and brings a higher vibration to all those who call on it for help. It heals emotional challenges and gently uncovers unconscious memories, embedded during emotional trauma. Violet has a very feminine, nurturing energy and fosters self-assurance. It can increase your intuition. Honoring this plant spirit will assist you in finding inner peace, and peace in your relationships with others.

The Physical Healing Properties

Violet is helpful in healing menstrual cramps. Take the essence in a dosage of 2 drops in water every hour until the pain subsides. You can also combine some of the essence with St. John's wort oil and massage it gently into the pelvic area.

For scratchy, watery eyes from allergens in the air, make a compress by moistening violet flowers and leaves with a little warmed water and placing them between layers of folded cotton cloth. Place this compress on the eyes for 10-minute intervals.

To ease the soreness of foot calluses, mix 10 drops of violet essence with equal amounts of warmed wheat germ oil, olive oil, and avocado oil. Massage it onto the affected area.

For drawing out the infection of boils on the skin, bathe with violet leaves or add 30 drops of the essence to bath water while consciously connecting to the plant spirit for help.

For swollen glands in the throat area, massage a mixture of violet essence and St. John's wort oil onto the affected area.

For swollen lymph and pelvic glands, massage a mixture of almond oil and drops of the essence onto the affected areas.

When there is acute inflammation as a result of chronic illness flare-up, take a dosage of 2 drops of violet essence every hour in water.

For jaw pain associated with dental work, lay a heavy compress on the inflamed area for an hour. To make this compress, mix 3 tablespoons of dried violet with 1 clove of crushed garlic and 2 tablespoons of olive oil. Use a mortar and pestle to make a loose paste. Lay the mixture between folded layers of cotton cloth.

To induce a restful sleep, surround yourself with fresh or dried violet flowers. To help with fatigue, take 12 drops of the essence per day between the hours of 11 a.m. and 1 p.m.

Wormwood
Plant Spirit Prayer

....

O Divine Providence, bring forth your spirit and help us heal the many wounds of our hearts. We seek your refuge in our lives. Bring us back to our wombs, to the place where we are one with God, to breathe in the fire of our souls.

....

Wormwood
(Artemisia absinthium)

My Experience with This Plant Spirit

When I call on the spirit of wormwood, a young maiden appears to me. She was born of the earth, a spirit of the lakes and rocks, and sits upon a rock at the edge of a lake, her hands lying gracefully at her sides. She is weeping for the loss of her lover and soul mate. Her face is hidden by her long, dark hair, and her feet burrow into the ground beneath her. She longs for him, searching for him and waiting for his return for an eternity.

As she gazes downward, she sees a silvery, luminescent wormwood plant growing between the rocks near her feet. She reaches for it and cradles it in her arms like a child. Her many tears fall upon the leaves of the plant, activating its spirit. Its magic, essence, and spiritual healing properties spring to life. The young maiden uses the plant spirit's essence to soothe her soul and call back her soul mate.

The Spiritual and Emotional Properties

Call on the spirit of wormwood when you are feeling disconnected from your heart and your inner sense of direction. When you hold the plant up to your heart chakra, the energy field surrounding the leaves permeates the heart membrane, increasing the energy flow between the organ itself and the subtle energy layers that surround it.

The loss of a soul mate or a life partner can be devastating. Call on the spirit of wormwood to help you work through the agony and find peace within. If you are having trouble in a relationship, call on wormwood to assist with healing at the heart level. Wormwood is also essential in healing from the loss of a child or from miscarriages. If you lose a child, cradling the plant itself in your arms can help nourish and heal the grief. When there is a miscarriage, many times the spirit of the unborn baby is still with the mother. The mother's healing revolves around letting the spirit go, giving the child permission to cross over to the spirit world to continue its journey. The spirit of wormwood will help the unborn baby find its way to the light. Call on wormwood to soothe irritability in children whatever the cause. It brings about playfulness and joviality.

Wormwood also aids in crossing over confused souls who have already separated from their physical bodies due to death, but are not yet ready to fully transition. If you place the plant and a white candle near the deceased's body and direct your intention, the soul will feel more at peace with the process of transitioning to the next stage of being.

Blessed by the spirit world, wormwood is highly regarded for its ability to provide protection and ward off evil spirits. On an energetic level, wormwood helps to align the crown chakra, the divine light of God, and clear the heart at the soul center, drawing energy downward and healing the physical body.

The Physical Healing Properties

Do not use when pregnant or nursing.

Wormwood eases the pain and inflammation of arthritis, rheumatic pain, and traumatic injury to the joints. It also helps to relieve back pain and tenderness from sciatica; make a mixture of the essence, warmed olive oil, and fresh parsley and massage it onto the affected area.

To heal the energy around astigmatism and vision problems, make a compress by taking wormwood leaves, moistening them with a little warm water, and placing them between folded layers of cotton cloth. Lay the compress over the closed eyes for no longer than 15 minutes. This is best done in the evening before you retire.

For a heart murmur, sleep with a wormwood plant (the whole plant, or whatever parts you are drawn to) over your heart at night; the glorious maiden will help it to heal.

For a vaginal yeast infection, take fresh chopped wormwood leaves, add a minuscule amount of warm water, and apply the mixture directly over the pubic bone between the hours of 11 a.m. and 12 noon. Leave it on for a half hour to an hour, depending upon the severity of the infection.

For a bladder infection, do the same as above, but place the leaves right over the pubic bone for an hour between 2 o'clock and 3 o'clock in the afternoon. (Note: if you work outside the home, do this whenever you can.)

For parasites in the digestive tract, wormwood essence helps to strengthen the boundary between the physical tissue and the parasites, assisting them in leaving the body. Place 4 drops of the essence in water and sip upon retiring.

YARROW
PLANT SPIRIT PRAYER

....

*O glorious melody, upon your strings, enchant us with divine
harmony. And unto us, heal the fruits of our many labors.*

....

Yarrow
(Achillea millefolium)

My Experience with This Plant Spirit

When I call on the spirit of yarrow, an innocent and gentle female being floats toward me. She is very ethereal, and wears a white satin scarf that presses against her long golden hair. She carries a harp, and appears very surreal and enchanting. Upon hearing the calls of the yarrow plant, she gracefully sets herself down in the midst of a lush green garden. The beautiful yarrow plants surrounding her immediately become hypnotized by her majestic presence. They share the many requests they have received, from the outside world, for medicinal and spiritual healing.

The spirit begins to play a song, a melody that will enable each request to be granted. As the music plays, the yarrow plants bend their stems toward the spirit, and the vibration of the music harmonizes the yarrow's incredible healing abilities.

The Spiritual and Emotional Properties

Call on the spirit of yarrow whenever you are feeling discouraged. It is the plant of support, and will foster that quality within you. Yarrow can help when you are feeling disillusioned with your life and work, incompetent, devalued, or unable to live up to others' expectations. Yarrow fosters an amazing sense of self-worth.

Along these lines, yarrow fosters emotional and mental strength. When you are feeling alone in a situation, or need to stand up for yourself, family, or friends, call on yarrow to assist. When you need to explain yourself in a difficult situation, call on yarrow to bring you courage, comfort, and ease. It helps you to confront the truth, of yourself and of others, and in taking responsibility for your feelings. It will help you get along with your neighbors.

Yarrow can guide you in your life, and guide you on the path of righteousness. It also helps to heal the emotional and spiritual energies around learning disabilities and Alzheimer's disease.

The Physical Healing Properties

Yarrow nourishes the energy of the spleen and pancreas. Take 3 drops of the essence under the tongue upon waking.

It is excellent in healing the energy around many different infections. For infections and poisons in the uterus and cervix, mix yarrow leaves with almond oil and massage it onto the pelvis.

For healing the energy around lung infections, pneumonia, and bronchitis, take 5–7 drops of yarrow essence in water each hour until the condition improves. Also massage an oil made from yarrow leaves, parsley, and olive oil onto the chest area.

Yarrow also is good for clearing infections in the ear canals. Make a mixture of warmed olive oil, 2–3 drops of yarrow essence, and 2–3 drops of red clover essence, and massage it around the ears.

To assist in healing pink eye, make a compress using yarrow leaves moistened with a little warm water and placed between folded layers of cotton cloth. Lay the compress on closed eyes for 20-minute intervals.

To treat throat infections such as tonsillitis, mix yarrow leaves and a few drops of yarrow essence with warmed castor oil and olive oil, and massage it onto the throat area.

Yarrow is useful in cleansing liver and gallbladder toxicity. Add a few drops of yarrow essence to warmed castor oil and massage it onto the affected areas, or use it with a castor oil pack.

It is also excellent for cleansing mercury toxicity and poisoning of the blood due to chemical toxicity; take 4 drops of the essence in water three times a day until the condition improves. Yarrow is a good lymphatic cleanser; take 2 drops in water when the need arises.

In general, yarrow can help cleanse environmental toxins both internally and in your energy field. There are a few ways to assist with this. You can make a spray mist using the essence, and moisten yourself with it. You can also sip 5–10 drops of the essence in water if you're feeling overwhelmed by the environment.

Yarrow helps to heal inflammation from various insect bites. Make a paste by mixing fresh yarrow leaves with a small amount of bentonite clay, and put it on the insect bite. Do not use this on open sores.

To heal the energy around fibroids and uterine cysts and cysts in the breast tissue, mix almond oil, yarrow leaves, and red clover, and massage it onto affected areas.

Adding a drop of the essence to your water will nourish the blood.

To help heal the pain of fibromyalgia, add some drops of the essence to your bath water, and also massage an oil made from yarrow leaves and warmed almond oil onto your body after bathing.

Yarrow is a good tonifier of the kidneys and adrenals. Place a few drops of the essence on your hands and touch the part of your back where kidneys and adrenals sit.

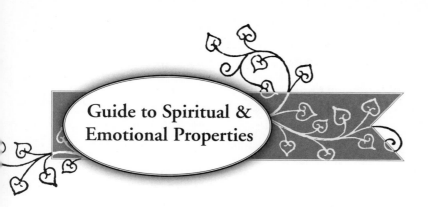

Guide to Spiritual & Emotional Properties

Abandonment: calendula,
   motherwort, pulsatilla
Abortion: pulsatilla
Abundance/Finances:
   dandelion, feverfew, poke
Abuse: dandelion, lamb's ear,
   mugwort
Acceptance: dandelion, lamb's
   ear, pulsatilla
Addictions: chamomile
Adoption: black cohosh
Alcoholism: chamomile,
   mugwort
Alzheimer's Disease (spiritual/
   emotional causes): yarrow
Ancestral Honoring: poke
Anger/Rage: chamomile,
   nettles, red clover,
   rosemary, sage

Animals: black cohosh, lilac,
   St. John's wort
Anxiety: marshmallow, poke
Authority: marshmallow
Balance: marshmallow
Boundaries: angelica,
   astragalus, calendula, poke
Celebration: blessed thistle
Ceremony: black cohosh
Child Labor: licorice
Child Loss: black cohosh,
   pulsatilla, St. John's wort,
   wormwood
Children/Babies: blessed thistle,
   calendula, lamb's ear,
   lemon balm, motherwort,
   mugwort, poke, rue, sage,
   wormwood
Codependency: blessed thistle

Comfort: astragalus, calendula, licorice, lilac, rosemary, yarrow

Communing with the Spirit World/Higher Power: lavender, mugwort, mullein, poke, rue

Community: clematis

Compassion: blessed thistle, clematis, pulsatilla

Compatibility: violet

Completion: blessed thistle, skullcap

Compromise: feverfew

Concentration: blessed thistle

Conflict: mullein, red clover

Confusion: chamomile, marshmallow, poke

Courage: lemon balm, pulsatilla, red clover, skullcap

Creativity: feverfew

Cultural/World Consciousness: clematis, licorice, poke

Deafness (trauma surrounding it): skullcap

Desire: mugwort

Direction: motherwort

Disconnection from Self/ Spirit: poke, skullcap, wormwood

Divine Mother: rosemary

Dreaming: poke, rue

Dying: mugwort, rue, wormwood

Elderly: blessed thistle

Emotional Stress: angelica, chamomile, marshmallow, mullein, violet

Empathy: nettles

Encouragement: mullein

Energy Field: angelica, lavender

Ethers (if one finds oneself "stuck" in the ethers): rue

Evil: angelica, black cohosh, feverfew, marshmallow, mugwort, rosemary, rue, sage, St. John's wort, wormwood

Expression: clematis, skullcap

Faith: mullein, poke

Fear: lemon balm, poke

Forgiveness: blessed thistle, lamb's ear, mullein, red clover, rosemary

Gentleness: violet

Grace: motherwort

Grief/Depression: chamomile, dandelion, feverfew, lavender, lemon balm, lilac, pulsatilla, red clover, rosemary, St. John's wort, wormwood

Grounding (spiritual/ emotional causes that may create the necessity for this): astragalus, nettles, rosemary, rue

Grudges: rosemary

Guidance: yarrow

Happiness: lavender, lilac, violet

Harmony: violet

Hatred: sage

Heartache: lemon balm

Honor: feverfew, red clover

Hope: licorice, pulsatilla

Injustice: lemon balm

Inner Child: calendula

Innocence: calendula
Insecurity: feverfew, skullcap,
	St. John's wort
Intuition: lamb's ear, sage,
	violet
Irritability: blessed thistle,
	wormwood
Jealousy/Envy: clematis,
	nettles, sage
Joy: calendula, lavender
Judgment: clematis, pulsatilla
Karma: lavender, licorice, sage
Light: feverfew, skullcap,
	violet, yarrow
Loneliness: calendula,
	rosemary, yarrow
Loss: astragalus, lamb's ear,
	lavender
Love: clematis, lamb's ear,
	lavender, lilac, poke,
	pulsatilla
Luck: poke, red clover
Magic: mullein
Menopause: lilac
Mental Hysteria: rue
Miracles: St. John's wort
Miscarriage: wormwood
Motivation: marshmallow,
	mugwort
Negative Thoughts: nettles,
	sage
Nervousness: angelica
Offering: black cohosh
Peace: blessed thistle, lamb's ear
Physical and Mental
	Disabilities: skullcap
Planetary Healing: poke
Play: calendula
Power: marshmallow
Pride: chamomile

Protection: angelica, black
	cohosh, blessed thistle,
	chamomile, feverfew,
	lamb's ear, marshmallow,
	motherwort, mugwort,
	poke, rosemary, rue, sage,
	St. John's wort, wormwood
Psychic Protection: angelica
Rape/Sexual Violence: lamb's
	ear, mugwort
Recovery: blessed thistle
Regret: feverfew, marshmallow,
	pulsatilla
Relationships: astragalus,
	blessed thistle, calendula,
	dandelion, feverfew,
	lavender, lilac, mullein,
	nettles, pulsatilla, red
	clover, sage, skullcap,
	violet, wormwood
Resentment: rosemary
Respect: astragalus, pulsatilla
Responsibility: pulsatilla, red
	clover
Resurrection: pulsatilla
Reverence: astragalus, black
	cohosh
Romance: lilac
Safety: calendula, chamomile,
	mullein
Secrets: skullcap
Self-esteem: clematis, St. John's
	wort
Selfishness: clematis, nettles
Sensuality/Sexuality: calendula,
	lamb's ear
Shame: red clover
Shyness: lamb's ear, skullcap

Societal Issues: clematis, lamb's ear, licorice, motherwort, mugwort

Soul Loss: astragalus

Spiritual Aspiration: lemon balm

Strength: angelica, dandelion, lemon balm, poke, red clover

Support: licorice, mullein, yarrow

Suppression: licorice

Surrendering: lamb's ear

Transition: lilac

Trauma: black cohosh, dandelion, lamb's ear, licorice, skullcap

Trust: poke

Truth: feverfew, skullcap, violet, yarrow

Unconscious Memories: violet

Understanding: dandelion, lamb's ear, pulsatilla, rosemary

Vengeance: sage

Violence: mugwort

Wars: licorice

Worry: mullein

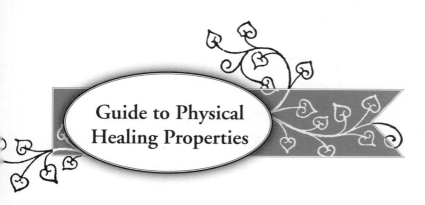

Guide to Physical Healing Properties

Adrenals: lavender, lemon balm, licorice, red clover, sage, yarrow

Allergies: lemon balm, pulsatilla, skullcap

Anemia: nettles, pulsatilla

Anxiety: astragalus, poke, St. John's wort

Arteries: dandelion, rue, St. John's wort

Arthritis: blessed thistle, mullein, nettles, rosemary, rue, wormwood

Autoimmune Disease: motherwort

Babies: lamb's ear

Bladder: black cohosh, blessed thistle, lavender, licorice, mugwort, wormwood

Blood: blessed thistle, clematis, nettles, red clover, rue, wormwood, yarrow

Blood Pressure: angelica, blessed thistle, dandelion, pulsatilla

Blood Sugar: lilac, marshmallow, rosemary

Bones: chamomile

Brain Aneurysms: motherwort

Brain Function: blessed thistle, calendula, marshmallow, motherwort, skullcap, wormwood

Breast Cancer: black cohosh

Breast Polyps: red clover

Bruises, Cuts, Wounds: astragalus, mugwort

Burns: lavender

Cancers (various): black cohosh, lamb's ear, red clover

Cervical Cancer: black cohosh

Cervical Dysplasia: dandelion

Chicken Pox/Shingles: pulsatilla

Cholesterol: rosemary

Circulation: blessed thistle, dandelion, lilac, lemon balm, marshmallow, red clover, rosemary, rue, sage

Colds: sage

Colic: angelica

Colon: marshmallow, motherwort, nettles, pulsatilla, sage

Constipation: clematis, lemon balm

Convulsions: astragalus, chamomile

Coughs: sage

Diaper Rash: chamomile, mullein

Diarrhea: chamomile, licorice

Digestive System: lavender, lemon balm, licorice, marshmallow, mugwort, nettles, sage

Dizziness: pulsatilla

Ears: feverfew, mugwort, St. John's wort, yarrow

Endocrine System: lamb's ear, rue

Energy: licorice, pulsatilla

Environmental Sensitivities/Toxicity: mullein, poke, yarrow

Eyes: blessed thistle, lamb's ear, lavender, mugwort, red clover, St. John's wort, violet, wormwood, yarrow

Fatigue: lemon balm

Feet: violet

Fertility: feverfew, astragalus

Fevers: angelica, feverfew

Fibroids/Cysts: black cohosh, red clover, yarrow

Fibromyalgia: yarrow

Fluid Retention: dandelion, mugwort

Fungus: clematis, lavender

Gallbladder: astragalus, blessed thistle, calendula, lilac, marshmallow, nettles, rue, St. John's wort, yarrow

Genital Herpes: clematis

Grounding (physical causes, in one's environment, that may create the necessity for this): sage, wormwood

Hay fever: skullcap

Headaches/Migraines: angelica, chamomile, dandelion, feverfew, pulsatilla, red clover, rosemary, skullcap, St. John's wort

Head Congestion: lemon balm, sage, St. John's wort

Heart: angelica, astragalus, black cohosh, blessed thistle, calendula, lamb's ear, motherwort, wormwood

Hemorrhoids: marshmallow, poke

Hernia: black cohosh

Hormones: astragalus, lilac

Immune System: astragalus, blessed thistle, motherwort, nettles, rosemary, St. John's wort, violet

Impotence: feverfew

Incontinence: mugwort

Indigestion: lavender, mugwort

Infections: red clover, yarrow

Influenza: chamomile, poke

Injuries: calendula

Insect Bites: skullcap, motherwort

Intestines: clematis, lemon balm, nettles

Jaw Pain: violet

Joints: calendula, mugwort, wormwood

Kidneys: blessed thistle, calendula, lavender, lemon balm, licorice, lilac, mugwort, mullein, red clover, rue, sage, yarrow

Learning Disabilities: feverfew

Liver: blessed thistle, feverfew, lavender, licorice, motherwort, nettles, pulsatilla, red clover, rosemary, rue, yarrow

Lungs (breathing, ailments, infections): dandelion, feverfew, lemon balm, licorice, lilac, mullein, nettles, poke, rosemary, sage, skullcap, St. John's wort, yarrow

Lyme Disease: rue

Lymphatic Cancer: red clover

Lymphatic System: lavender, lilac, motherwort, nettles, violet, wormwood, yarrow

Menopause: lilac

Menstruation: angelica, black cohosh, blessed thistle, lavender, lilac, mugwort, nettles, pulsatilla, sage, skullcap, violet

Mental Illness: black cohosh, poke

Miscarriage: clematis

Morning Sickness: licorice, sage

Mucous: dandelion, lemon balm, mugwort, St. John's wort, wormwood

Multiple Sclerosis: mullein

Muscles: calendula, chamomile, motherwort, poke, sage

Nausea: chamomile, feverfew, rue

Nerve Pain: calendula, feverfew

Nervous System: angelica, astragalus, black cohosh, motherwort, pulsatilla, St. John's wort

Nosebleeds: black cohosh

Pancreas: lavender, lilac, marshmallow, motherwort, yarrow

Parasites: calendula, marshmallow, poke, red clover, wormwood

Poison Ivy/Oak: chamomile

Pregnancy/Birthing: red clover

Prickly Heat: mullein

Rape/Sexual Violence: lamb's ear

Reproductive System (males): angelica, lamb's ear

Rest/Sedation: motherwort, skullcap, St. John's wort, violet

Scar Tissue: motherwort

Sciatica: St. John's wort, wormwood

Seizures: clematis, lamb's ear

Sexual Energy: calendula

Sexually Transmitted Diseases: red clover

Sinus: dandelion, lavender, licorice, mugwort, nettles, red clover, rosemary

Skeletal/Muscular System: blessed thistle

Skin Rashes/Diseases: chamomile, clematis, marshmallow, mullein, violet

Smoking: lemon balm, rosemary

Spinal Column: motherwort, St. John's wort

Spleen: lavender, marshmallow, motherwort, rosemary, wormwood, yarrow

Stomach: astragalus, nettles, rosemary, rue

Strength: nettles

Stress: black cohosh, lavender, lemon balm

Swollen Glands: sage, violet, wormwood

Throat: astragalus, feverfew, lemon balm, poke, rosemary, sage, skullcap, St. John's wort, yarrow

Throat Cancer: red clover

Thymus: blessed thistle, calendula

Thyroid: lamb's ear, St. John's wort

Tonsillitis: skullcap

Toothache: chamomile

Tumors: motherwort

Ulcers: marshmallow, motherwort

Uterus: angelica, black cohosh, calendula, lemon balm, pulsatilla, rue, skullcap, St. John's wort, violet, yarrow

Vaginal Discomfort: skullcap

Varicose Veins: sage

Weakness: mullein

Worms: clematis, feverfew, red clover, wormwood

Yeast Infections/Candida: clematis, lavender, lilac, red clover, wormwood

To Write to the Author

If you wish to contact the author or would like more information about this book, please write to the author in care of Llewellyn Worldwide and we will forward your request. Both the author and publisher appreciate hearing from you and learning of your enjoyment of this book and how it has helped you. Llewellyn Worldwide cannot guarantee that every letter written to the author can be answered, but all will be forwarded. Please write to:

Laura Silvana
⁒ Llewellyn Worldwide
2143 Wooddale Drive, Dept. 978-07387-1863-7
Woodbury, Minnesota 55125-2989, U.S.A.

Please enclose a self-addressed stamped envelope for reply,
or $1.00 to cover costs. If outside U.S.A., enclose
international postal reply coupon.

Many of Llewellyn's authors have websites with additional information and resources. For more information, please visit our website at http://www.llewellyn.com.

Related Links

During the writing of various parts of this book, I used some special sage to smudge, which I purchased from a few different places. I want to be of support to these family businesses, especially because of the love, hard work, and belief they put into their products.

- Colleen Heminger-Cordell and her family grow their own sage and make most of the products that they sell. You can visit her on her website at http://www.indiangifts.com. You can also email her at colleen@indiangifts.com.

- Also check out a very cool site, http://www.coyotescorner.com. They sell everything from sage to drums to clothing.